SpringerBriefs in Computer Science

For further volumes:
http://www.springer.com/series/10028

Md. Atiqur Rahman Ahad

Motion History Images for Action Recognition and Understanding

 Springer

Md. Atiqur Rahman Ahad
Department of Applied Physics, Electronics and
  Communication Engineering
University of Dhaka
Dhaka
Bangladesh

ISSN 2191-5768   ISSN 2191-5776 (electronic)
ISBN 978-1-4471-4729-9   ISBN 978-1-4471-4730-5 (eBook)
DOI 10.1007/978-1-4471-4730-5
Springer London Heidelberg New York Dordrecht

Library of Congress Control Number: 2012950858

Printed on acid-free paper

Springer is part of Springer Science+Business Media (www.springer.com)

This book is dedicated to—
my wife Shahera Hossain (Ruba) &
my lovely daughter Rumaisa Fatima!

Foreword

It is commonly observed that what used to be science fiction eventually becomes engineering fact. This is certainly the case for human–computer interaction technologies, where speech recognition and synthesis, gesture recognition, face recognition, facial expression analysis, and other technologies that were introduced to many people in sci-fi settings have become, or are in the process of becoming, a part of our daily lives. These transitions are not the result of magic potion or of mad scientists alone in their labs, but of many researchers proposing and testing methods that, bit by bit, bring the technologies closer to reality. These communities of researchers are largely driven by what is possible, what is needed, and what is interesting.

The topic of human behavior analysis has received a great amount of attention in recent years, due to the increasing computational power available to analyze video streams as well as the interest in applications of action and gesture recognition in security and surveillance, human–computer interaction, gaming, and other areas. Motion History Images (MHIs), first introduced by Davis and Bobick in the 1990s, provide certain advantages in representational power and efficiency that have proved to be quite useful in the recognition of human movement, action, and activity. In addition to its effective practical use, there is an elegance in the MHI representation that makes the method a valuable tool for learning and thinking about human movement recognition.

Though still a young researcher with a long, promising career of contributions ahead of him, Md. Atiqur Rahman Ahad has a substantial background of experience in optics, image processing, and computer vision with a focus on human activity analysis, developing and assessing methods for representing, and recognizing a range of spatio-temporal events. With a solid track record of relevant conference and journal publications, Ahad is well positioned to reintroduce the concept of Motion History Images to perhaps a new generation of researchers and system builders, who—armed with considerably better tools than in the 1990s—may use this as a starting point to push the boundaries of what is possible in human activity analysis and perhaps in other areas of motion-based video interpretation. Ahad provides an overview of the MHI method and discusses variations of the method, technical challenges that still need to be addressed, a range of applications for which the technique is well suited, and datasets available to researchers working in the area. The tutorial level approach makes this book accessible to students new to the area, which also provides a useful summary for experienced researchers in the field.

I encourage readers to approach the book with the question in mind, how can we build on this? That is, if we understand the strengths and limitations of the MHI approach to representing and recognizing activity, we are better prepared to explore the follow-up methods that may make robust, real-time human activity analysis commonplace tomorrow. It is possible; it is needed; and, as this book may convince you, it is certainly interesting.

Santa Barbara, CA, August 2012   Matthew Turk

Preface

This book is about the Motion History Image (MHI) and its developments. Broadly, it falls in the arena of computer vision and image processing. On a smaller scale, the book is on action/activity/gesture/gait recognition and human behavior analysis. It is known that human action analyses and recognition are challenging problems due to large variations in human motion and appearance, camera viewpoint, and various other issues related to environment settings. Though the field of action and activity representation and recognition is relatively old, yet it is not well understood by the student and research communities. Some important but common motion recognition problems are even now unsolved properly by the computer vision community. However, in the past decade, a number of good approaches have been proposed and evaluated subsequently by many researchers. Among those methods, MHI method and its variants get significant attention from many researchers in the computer vision field due to their better robustness and performance.

This book attempts to reduce the gap of information and materials on comprehensive outlook—through various strategies from scratch to mainly the MHI method and its variants, challenges, and applications. This book targets the students and researchers who have knowledge on image processing at a basic level and would like to explore more on this area and do research. The step-by-step methodologies will encourage one to move forward for a comprehensive knowledge on computer vision for recognizing various human actions, with the aid of the concept of the motion history images and its variants.

Some good features of this book are:

- No book is available as per my knowledge that covers action recognition considering the MHI in a comprehensive manner in the arena of computer vision.
- Both students (who have basic knowledge on image processing) and researchers can use this book for their academic learning and research purposes.
- The book covers the MHI—a state-of-the-art method on recognition approach and it can guide a fellow on how to move forward.

- This book can be used as a textbook (full or partial) for students of level-2 or above, who have studied basic image processing already in an earlier session—both for undergraduate and graduate students.

The book comprises four chapters. Chapter 1 has background on action recognition. Chapter 2 presents some aspects of action recognition. As the book is targeted to be a shortened one, not much details have been covered in these chapters. In Chap. 3, the core chapter of on the *Motion History Image* method and its variants, detailed analysis, and variants are covered. This chapter illustrates on how to advance from one method to another, how to improve an existing method and mitigate its shortcoming, how to employ an approach in various other applications, etc. Therefore, this chapter is highly beneficial for an enthusiastic researcher or student to move forward. Finally, Chap. 4 covers some databases that are employed for the MHI method. Due to page limits, detailed issues are not covered but referred for further reading. I hope that this book will have an impact, serve the community in a positive direction, and help people to learn.

For any query on this book or corrections, please write to me. I am thankful to my teachers, co-researchers, and students. All images are produced, except some of these which are taken with the kind permission of Springer Science+Business Media B.V. A few images are created by Upal Mahbub. I am grateful to Ahmed Boudissa for his kind time to check the book. I specially thank Simon Rees of *Springer* for his constant support to finish the book.
Thank you all!

Fukuoka, Japan, August 2012   Md. Atiqur Rahman Ahad

Email: atiqahad@univdhaka.edu
Preferred websites:
http://IJEI.org
http://ICIEV.org
http://IJCVSP.com
http://benjapan.org/IJE
http://benjapan.org/ICEAB

Acknowledgments

I am much grateful to my *sensei*—Seiji Ishikawa, *Kyushu Institute of Technology, Japan*. I am thankful to J. K. Tan (*Kyushu Institute of Technology, Japan*), H. Kim (*Kyushu Institute of Technology, Japan*), Z. H. Mahmood (*University of Dhaka, Bangladesh*), and other teachers who helped me throughout my tenure as a student.

A great number of researchers, academicians, and students were behind the scene to motivate me to write this book and I am thankful to them from the core of my heart. I thank Upal Mahbub, of *Bangladesh University of Engineering and Technology, Bangladesh* who produced a few images for the book. I am thankful to my parents—none can replace them, their efforts. Parents are tremendous! I can never forget the efforts of my beloved mother who single-handedly managed and supported after my father died at an early age. I am ever grateful to her.

Finally, Shahera Hossain—to whom I am extremely thankful for her support and encouragement. She has always supported me even when she was in hospital and passing through bad patches.

Contents

Acronyms

3D-MHM	3D Motion History Model
AEI	Action Energy Image
AME	Average Motion Energy
DEI	Dominant Energy Image
DMHI	Directional Motion History Image
EMHI	Edge Motion History Image
FDHI	Frame Difference History Image
GEI	Gait Energy Image
GEnI	Gait Entropy Image
GHI	Gait History Image
GMI	Gait Moment Energy
GMM	Gaussian Mixture Model
HMHH	Hierarchical Motion History Histogram
HMM	Hidden Markov Model
HOG	Histogram of Oriented Gradients
ITS	Intelligent Transport System
LBP	Local Binary Pattern
MDI	Moment Deviation Image
MEH	Motion Energy Histogram
MEI	Motion Energy Image
MEV	Motion Energy Volume
MFH	Motion Flow History
MGO	Motion Gradient Orientation
MHI	Motion History Image
MHV	Motion History Volume
MMHI	Multi-level Motion History Image
MMS	Mean Motion Shape
PCA	Principal Component Analysis
SEI	Silhouette Energy Image
SHI	Silhouette History Image
SIFT	Scale-Invariant Feature Transform

SURF	Speeded-Up Robust Features
tMHI	*timed*-Motion History Image
VMHI	Volumetric Motion History Image
VMT	Volume Motion Template
XYT	Space(X,Y)–Time(T) Volume

Chapter 1
Introduction

Abstract Action and activity representation and recognition are very demanding research areas in computer vision and man–machine interaction. Although plenty of researches have been done in the field of action recognition, it remains still immature and not enough. This chapter overviews various issues for human activity recognition and then introduces the MHI method. The following chapters will elaborate on these concepts.

1.1 Introduction

As this book is about action or activity analysis and recognition by the Motion History Image method, it is important to define human action or activity in the field of computer vision. Action or activity or gesture or related terms are used interchangeably in the literature. There is so far no profound nomenclature that can differentiate these terms. Therefore, it is necessary to define these terms and then explain the importances of action/activity recognition. The recognition and interpretation of human- or robot-induced actions and activities have gained considerable interest in the computer vision, robotics and AI communities [35]. We will see that action recognition and behavior analysis have numerous applications.

An automatic scene understanding system that include the interpretation of the observed actions such as *what* actions are executed, *where* these actions are seen, *who* is/are the subject(s), and a *prediction of what* the observed individuals' intentions might be given their present behavior [35]—are in the demanding list. However, we are still far behind to accomplish this kind of reality through the algorithms of computer vision and robotics. This field becomes multidisciplinary—covering computer vision, image processing, robotics, control, psychology, cognition, neurobiology, pattern recognition, and so on. However, due to the lack of some comprehensive approaches to solve various problems, covering multimodality, and experimenting various realistic scenes—the action recognition and behavior analysis remains in its

Md. A. R. Ahad, *Motion History Images for Action Recognition and Understanding*,
SpringerBriefs in Computer Science, DOI: 10.1007/978-1-4471-4730-5_1,
© Md. Atiqur Rahman Ahad 2013

infancy even though researchers are on it for a few decades. However, recent developments and coordinated collaborative works are changing the scene in a faster pace than in the remote past. We begin this book with this hope that this book brings some concrete and essential knowledge for these communities and help thereby.

1.2 Action/Activity: Nomenclature

This section presents various nomenclatures of action or activity based on the existing literature. At the top and intermediate levels—*action* and *activity*, respectively—are situations in which knowledge other than the immediate motion is required to generate the appropriate label [492]. The most primitive level, however, is *movement*—a motion whose execution is consistent and easily characterized by a definite space–time trajectory in some feature space. Such consistency of execution implies that for a given viewing condition there is consistency of appearance.

While extracting conceptual descriptions from image sequences, Nagel [34] mentions a hierarchy of—

- Change—is a discernible *motion* in a sequence.
- Event—is a *change* which is considered as a *primitive* of a more complex descriptions.
- Verb—describes some *activity*.
- Episode— describes *complex motions* that may involve several actions.
- History—is an extended sequence of related activities.

On the other hand, Bobick [31] presents another hierarchy of—

- Movement—is a predictable motion that can be defined by a space–time trajectory; no knowledge other than motion is needed.
- Activity—is composed of sequences of movements.
- Action—involves semantic knowledge related to the context of motion.

—as different levels of abstraction, which is later reiterated by [561]. Based on the above two taxonomies, Gonzalez et al. [32] present another nomenclature, having the following divisions,

- Movement—a change of human posture or place between consecutive frames.
- Action—is defined as a process of human performing that has a significance based on an application;
- Activity—is defied as a sequence of one or more human actions.
- Situation—means that these actions will be learned so that their recognition can be properly achieved in a later stage.

In another work [33], action vocabularies are derived from motion stream, where they finally find two key primitives, namely—

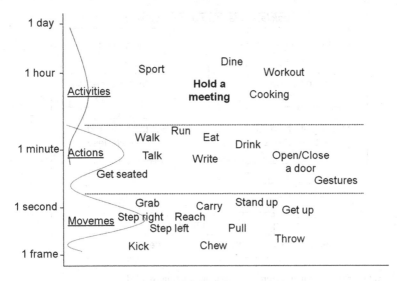

Fig. 1.1 Hierarchy of action–activities by Fanti [177]

- Action primitives—are similar to *verbs* in manually derived *verbs* and *adverbs* vocabularies. In terms of linguistic grammar, action primitives could be considered *terminals*.
- Parent behaviors—represent sequences of action primitives. These are similar to *verb graphs* in *verbs* and *adverbs*. In terms of linguistic grammars, behavior primitives could be considered *non-terminals*.

In this case, from a motion stream, motion segments are achieved after some preprocessing steps. Spatio-temporal Isomap is constructed. From the Isomap, we can have the following two branches:

- Spatio-temporal Isomap → Action embedding → Action units by clustering → Motion interpolation → **Action Primitives**
- Spatio-temporal Isomap → Behavior embedding → Behavior units by clustering → Action linking → **Behavior Primitives**

Fanti in his work [177] schematically presents a hierarchy of action–activities. It is shown in Fig. 1.1. The layers are [177]—

- Movemes—are atomic motions which are learned without supervision from data, and do not necessarily possess a verbal description. Its duration covers up to a few frames and it may overlap with some simple gestures where a slight movement of body parts is involved.
- Actions—are shorter events, comprised movemes that, joined together probabilistically, yield an activity. An action lasts typically for a few seconds. Some repetitive events such as walking or running are also considered as actions, because the elementary cycle that is repeated fits the definition of action.

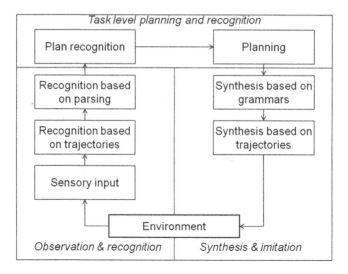

Fig. 1.2 Action recognition at different level of abstraction by [35]

- Activity—resides at the highest layer, extends over an extended period of time.

  Another action hierarchy [35] adopt the following terms–

- Action primitives or motor primitives—are used for atomic entities out of which actions are built. The granularity of the primitives often application dependent; e.g., in robotics, motor primitives are often understood as sets of motor control commands that are used to generate an action by the robot.
- Actions—are used for a sequence of action primitives needed to accomplish a task. Most of the researches are concentrated in this region.
- Activities—are larger-scale events that typically depend on the context of the environment, interacting humans or objects.

    The following example enhance the above hierarchy. For a sport like tennis, *action primitives* could be, e.g., forehand, backhand, run left, run right. *Action* is used for a sequence of action primitives needed to return a ball. Based on action primitives, returning a ball could be varied—therefore, different combinations produce different actions (in this case, return a ball). Finally, playing tennis is an *activity*!

    Reference [35] reviews on action recognition where they present different approaches taken to-date for dealing with actions at different level of complexity (Fig. 1.2), namely,

- Observation, interpretation and recognition of action, e.g.,

  - Scene-based interpretation
  - Recognizing actions based on body parts
  - Recognizing actions without using body parts

  – Decoupling actions into action *primitives* and interpreting actions with
    grammars
- Action learning, synthesis and imitation
- Task-level planning and recognition

Note that, none of the taxonomies considers emotion, affective computing, cognition, etc. Incorporating these areas are necessary. Although several attempts have been made to distinguish these terms—none of these definitions has gotten enough attention in the vision community. In this subsection, hence, we will present important definitions that are already existing in various sources.

1.2.1 Atomic Actions

Usually, a video clip is processed as a block or a full action or activity for recognition and analysis, and is assigned a single action label [149]. However, our human vision system proves that simple actions can be recognized almost instantaneously [149], which is not the case for computer vision system. Usually, atomic action units are action dependent [149]. Moreover, it is crucial to define the points or frame from where the composition into the basic action units can be done [149, 150, 178].

Actom:
Regarding atomic or primitive action, Gaidon et al. [150] called it *actom* where an action is decomposed into sequences of key atomic action units. An *actom* is a short *atomic action*, identified by its central temporal location around what discriminative visual information is present [150]. These actoms are key components of short duration, whose sequence is the characteristic of an action. However, it is challenging to get these actoms or achieve the decomposition of actions. For example, different viewpoints, poses, multisubjects in the scene, etc. may turn this decomposition a difficult task.

Action Snippet:
Another term for action primitive is proposed, which is called *action snippet*. It is composed of short sequences of a few to 10 frames of a video sequence [149].

Basic Motion:
Another term but not well-defined by [378] is called *basic action*. It is the smallest action unit.

Fundamental Gesture:
Various *gestures* may also be in the arena of the fundamental action units. Some gestures are simply atomic actions. For example, Iahara et al. [376] consider the bottom-level action unit as *fundamental gesture*. Kahol et al. [520, 521] segment an action into smaller action units and they call these as *gesture*.

Basis Vector:

Reference [59] defines the action primitives as an optimal sparse linear combination of the learned basis vectors (action primitives) to represent the actions.

Actem:

In speech recognition, phonemes have demonstrated their efficacy to model the words of a language. While they are well defined for languages, their extensions to human actions are not straightforward. Kulkarni et al. [30] study such an extension and propose an unsupervised framework to find phoneme-like sub-action units, which they call actemes, using 3D data and without any prior assumptions.

Dyneme:

Green and Guan [29] propose the use of 35 *dynemes* which form the basic units of human actions or skills. The dynemes are defined in terms joint angles. An HMM model is used for action recognition.

Kineteme:

Another work [28] defines *kinetemes* on the joint angle space of human motion. These kinetemes form the basic unit of a human activity language. Using these kinetemes and language grammar like rules, the authors propose to construct any complex human action.

Movemes:

Movemes is introduced [179] as linear dynamical systems over which an Hidden Markov Model (HMM) is learned for recognition. Fanti in his work [177] defines it more elaborately and in the action/activity taxonomy, we present movemes too.

The term *action primitives* is used by many [22, 33, 35]. The neurobiological findings motivate researchers to identify a set of action primitives that allow [35],

- Representation of the visually perceived action, and
- Motor control for imitation.

1.2.2 Action

Action can be defined as those body movements, which are simple and may be considered as the smallest or basic element of something done by a human being. Of course, an action should be done by a single subject. An action can also be composed of some basic actions or atomic actions or action primitives [150]. Now, how to define an atomic or primitive action? It is an arena where it might be very difficult to draw a clear line to separate these.

1.2.3 Activity

On the other hand, an *activity* is something that is a combination of several basic or simple actions. It can be done by a single or multisubject. Simple action versus complex action are also defined. The latter can be called as activity too. However, some behaviors of a human being or a group of people can be activity or combinations of activities.

Action or activity comes in various flavors—some actions are too slow that for a few consecutive frames, it may appear as static. Some actions are prolonged (e.g., a video of a driver who is driving in a straight road and where he may not need to move the steering or driving wheel of the car for a period, and hence, though the person is driving, it may not give proper clue for a while). Some actions cover the movement of the entire body (running, jumping jack, etc.), in some cases, only the upper body part (waving hands, boxing, shooting) or lower body part (kicking a ball). Drinking a cup of coffee versus riding a horse demonstrate how much different actions can be in terms of moving regions and the amount of moving information. So, action or activity has many dimensions and all are not covered under a single method yet! An action recognition framework should incorporate contextual information, detection of objects (*cup* for the case of 'drinking coffee'; *soccer ball* for the case of 'kicking a ball'; etc.).

1.3 Various Dimensions of Action Recognition

We defined action or activity. We will define action recognition and its various dimensions. The term *recognition* is meant to determine whether a given input (e.g., in this case, a video or some consecutive frames) is similar to another data from a data bank. If the input action representation finds significant similarity with another action with some probability—based on some pattern recognition approach, then we can say that the input action is recognized, else not. In another term, action recognition is 'understanding the body's movements over time' [47]. However, it is not easy to recognize an action from a raw video. From an input video, some sort of representations or features should be produced. Thereafter, these will be compared with all datasets or data bank. Apart from the task of having a better presentation or a smart feature vector for an action, the *pattern recognition* part is very important for a smart recognition system. So, recognizing an action is not a trivial task. Choosing an appropriate *machine learning* approach is important after having a smart feature vector for an action. The Motion History Image (MHI) representation is a smart but simple action-representation strategy and in this book, we will detail on this approach. From this concept, one can rationalize and understand other approaches for action recognition.

Understanding and recognizing actions are simply difficult tasks. Actions are typically dynamic and may not be easily recognized by simple attention to single moments in time [632]. The overhead related to dynamic scenes, cluttered background, changing in illuminations, variations in subjects, varieties of action classes, etc. turn action recognition into a more complicated task. Moreover, action recognition is complicated by the variation between people and even between instances of a single person [632]. We will notice that there are a number of different datasets covering diverse types of actions or gestures or activities—and not a single method can perform well in most of the datasets. Till date, the performances in terms of recognizing diverse actions are limited to some specific datasets and with prior constraints. Therefore, ample of tasks ahead to accomplish to develop smarter approaches for action/activity recognition. For example, a successful action recognition approach should have the ability to remove any explicit or implicit background smartly [632].

1.3.1 Applications

Action recognition and related fields have various important applications. *Looking at People* is a promising field within computer vision with many applications [37]. Some of these are—

- Video surveillance in various places for security management.
- Sports video analysis and evaluation.
- Biomechanics and physical therapy.
- Gesture-based interactive games.
- Action understanding by robots and intelligent systems to support in various applications.
- Smart-house, hospitals, rehabilitation center, assisted living, etc.
- Entertainment industry—movies, 3D TV, animation.
- Monitoring crowded scenes, e.g., monitoring people fighting, falling person detection, etc.
- Intelligent transport systems for safety driving.
- Detecting suspicious behavior, e.g., fence climbing, attacking, fighting.
- Robot learning and control.
- Video annotation.
- Motion segmentation.
- Emotion analysis.
- Automated mental/cognitive development.
- Gesture recognition.
- Gait recognition and analysis.
- Advanced human–computer interaction (HCI).

1.3.2 Action Recognition is Difficult: Why?

According to the literature [59], some important aspects of human actions and motion imagery that turn action recognition into difficult task are presented below:

- **Each action has varied dimensionality and data redundancy**:
  Actions vary in terms of dimensionality and overlapping. Once an action video is subdivided to compute spatio-temporal patches, we may get high-dimensional

data samples and data redundancy may occur from the high temporal sampling rate, allowing relatively smooth frame-to-frame transitions, hence the ability to observe the same object many times (not considering shot boundaries) [59].

- **Periodicity of actions**:
  Actions may have an associated periodicity of movements. Some actions are repetitive in nature, or some actions has overlapping in terms of more than one simple action. For example, waving hands, running, continuous standing and sitting actions, etc. Hence, for some methods, periodic actions become redundant and difficult to recognize. For overlapping patches, any spatio-temporal features or attributes may be very similar, and will be accounted multiple times with relatively low variation [59].

- **Human activities are very diverse compare to normal actions**:
  As defined above—activities are mainly composed or defined by sequences or linear combinations of actions or basic actions. So, an activity may have different dimensions which can be difficult to put into a same framework for action classification. For example, playing basketball or soccer, swimming, throwing something, etc., may be different in different situations or performed by different subjects. Hence, it becomes difficult to recognize if an activity has diversity like this.

- **Some actions/activities share common movements**:
  Some actions may seem similar and very difficult to distinguish. For example, the famous KTH dataset [651] has six action classes—having running and jogging as two different action classes. It is noticeable that some running action by some subjects look like jogging by another and even for a human subject—it becomes difficult to classify running and jogging actions with 100 % recognition rate—let alone by a method. The reality is that some torso and arms movements may be very similar for both actions. Therefore, there are spatio-temporal structures that are shared between actions. While one would think that a person running moves faster than a person jogging, in reality it could be the exact opposite (consider race-walking) [59].

  This phenomena suggests that our natural ability to classify actions is not based only on local observations (e.g., torso and arm movements) or global observations (e.g., person's velocity) but on local and global observations [59]. Blake and Shiffrar and their recent psychological research indicate that the perception of human actions are a combination of spatial hierarchies of the human body along with motion regularities.

- **Relationships between actions are difficult to separate**:
  It is really difficult for most of the methods to recognize continuous actions, because selecting the splitting point or boundary of two different but sequential actions is challenging. Most of the cases, we have separate action classes and we evaluate them separately—hence, the recognition results are reasonably acceptable.

- **Variations in illumination**:
  Lighting conditions are usually taken fixed for most of the datasets. So, indoor and constant illuminations are producing easier action datasets for evaluation. However, in reality, actions or activities should be taken outdoor where as per the time of the day (sunlight in the morning versus noon versus afternoon) or weather (cloudy versus rainy versus sunny day)—the lighting conditions vary to a large extent; and this variations in lighting make the recognition process a tougher one.

- **Variability in the video data**:
  While important applications (e.g., surveillance video) consist of a single acquisition protocol; and the action data to classify is often recorded in a large variety of scenarios, leading to different viewing angles, resolution, and general quality. An example of these sorts of dataset is the YouTube dataset [124, 126], where various variabilities are present. It is taken by various research groups.

- **Multicamera system**:
  It means lots of video sequences and in different angles, and hence very difficult to synchronize and recognize.

- **View-invariance issue**:
  It is still difficult to handle, as most of the approaches are based on view-based system where a single camera takes images from a fixed point—mainly nonmoving camera, and occlusions and other problems are inherited in view-based system. To have view-invariance system, some approaches exploit multicameras along with more complex which are usually more taxing. However, view-invariance datasets usually consist of trivial action classes.

- **Execution rate**:
  Another challenge is the execution rate. To have a smart real-time system for action recognition with variable classes is still very limited or inexistent in terms of satisfactory recognition results. Real-time analysis is necessary for some applications—but many methods require prior information, modeling, feature vectors, etc.—which make it impossible for real-time applications.

- **Anthropometry of subjects**:
  Almost all datasets have no significant variability in terms of size, height, gender, dress effect, etc. of actors. Usually, actors are male, adult, similar heights and short range of ages.

- **Dataset issue**:
  As different methods use different datasets—it is difficult to rationalize which method is comparatively more suitable than another one. Although we have some benchmark datasets which are widely exploited—the detailed features (e.g., timing, limitations, processing speed, etc.) of those algorithms are not known.

- **Inside smart-house or rehabilitation center**:
  Action recognition in smart-house or rehabilitation center is difficult but it becomes very much demanding, especially in those countries where number of aged population is increasing dramatically. For example, in 2007, Japan had 20 % population

above 65 years of age; and in year 2030—this number will jump up to 25 % of its total population. In China, by 2050, 30 % of the citizens will be over 60 years of age (Source: *Shanghai Daily*, 22 June 2012, p. A6). This sort of situations are going to be prominent in some other countries as well. Therefore, to support these growing numbers of elderly people—especially, those who will be needing to stay in hospitals or rehabilitation centers—we need to develop smarter systems so that they can be supported by robots or intelligent machines, as well as, monitored by surveillance camera systems to avoid accidents, and other problems.

- **ITS**:
  For Intelligent Transport Systems (ITS), action recognition is important and various car companies are spending funds for this purpose. But this is much more challenging because the environment is outdoor, hence varied illumination and sometimes, very poor lighting. Presence of other moving vehicles as well as multiple people, mainly pedestrian make it very difficult. Image depth analysis is also required. Moreover, involvement of moving cameras (within a vehicle) in a higher speed is another challenging area.

- **Low-resolution issue**:
  Low-resolution and poor quality videos are difficult to process.

- **Occlusion issue**:
  Partially occluded actions are not tried much for recognition let alone to have smart approaches. Presence of cluttered background in a video scene makes the action analysis and recognition into a more difficult task. For example, in a bus stand or a busy area, determining whether someone falls down on the floor or searching something, or showing gestures or fighting, etc. are really difficult to identify and then recognize.

- **Problems with model-based approaches**: Loose clothing, self-occlusions, inaccurate body models due to dress effect, unavailability of limbs (dress effect may turn a person as a cylindrical shape, instead of body parts as arms, legs, and head), having limb-like structures (which might be recognized as a limb wrongfully) turns model-based approaches into jeopardy. So, recognition becomes difficult because one cannot model a moving actor in a reasonable manner.

Therefore, plenty of avenues remain wide open or not filled yet, and new researchers can dig into these challenging but important areas for a better future.

1.3.3 Some Assumptions on Action Recognition

While studying action recognition and analysis, we often consider a number of assumptions that may hinder the performance in real-life situations. But we have to consider these as no single method till date, that can perform significantly well in every situation. Some of the assumptions that we consider based on the situations are—

- Usually, we consider constant lighting situation and hence take videos in indoor environment to keep away from varying illumination.
- Static background is considered so that it becomes easier for background subtraction or frame-to-frame subtraction. However, for a dynamic background where apart from the target foreground scene, there may be some moving objects in the background, the extraction of foreground becomes difficult and false positives are higher. Therefore, for a scene with dynamic background, smarter background subtraction approaches are employed.
- Uniform background is considered. A scene having cluttered background is difficult to analyze.
- Camera parameters are usually known.
- Static camera(s) are used. Moving camera poses more challenges.
- Moving subject moves perpendicular to the optical axis of the camera, i.e., parallel to the camera-plane. Therefore, a person moving or doing an action towards the optical axis of a camera or in diagonal directions are not considered in most of the cases. We can notice after looking into various datasets that a walking person is always walking from one corner to another—perpendicular direction to the optical axis of the camera; or the moving subject is always facing towards the camera. Only exception is in the case of multicamera systems where the same action from the perpendicular direction of the optical axis of a camera will be very much different from another camera facing in $90°$ or $45°$.
- Usually, *real-time* applications are not considered initially because it is difficult for most of the cases to apply a method in real-time or pseudo-real-time applications, mainly due to the time-computational cost for various algorithms.
- Sometimes, we use special hardware (e.g., FPGA) or faster PC with more memory.
- For some methods, body parts or poses are known. Various models are designed.
- Subjects are not varied much. For example, most of the subjects who play in making the action scenes are adult and mostly male with regular costumes or in some cases, special dresses. There are not enough variations in terms of gender, height, race, body size, clothing, cultural variations, etc.
- Some markers (active or passive markers) are used in some cases for pose estimation. By tracking body markers, one can recognize human posture and this approach is called intrusive/interfering-based technique. It is however, difficult to track the marker-based feature points, especially any self-occlusion or missing points create constraints.
- In a few cases, special dresses are used to avoid texture or to show distinct object color from background. Tight-fitting cloths are used in motion capture system.
- Subjects are confined in limited areas—for example, indoor, or for the case of outdoor scenes, in limited and less varied places to avoid dynamic background, multiple moving objects, shadow, cluttered environment. Moreover, the floor is usually considered flat plane, though a few papers consider an action in different situations or backgrounds.
- Usually, a single person at a time demonstrates actions. However, in some cases, two persons interact in handshaking, hugging, fighting, crossing each other, etc. Note that algorithms related to multiperson detection and tracking are challenging,

especially in those cases where occlusions cause problem in extracting the moving object.

- Occlusions are avoided. There can be diverse sources of occlusions. A bar or tree can occlude a full body for a while, a moving car can partially occlude the lower part of a moving person, another person crossing in front of the target subject can occlude fully and it may cause difficulties in tracking the target person. Apart from these occlusions, the motion overwriting or self-occlusion causes problem. Let us define the motion self-occlusion. If a person is sitting down and stand up again, for some cases, it is motion self-occlusion as the prior motion information (i.e., the sitting down movement) is overwritten by the late movement of standing up. This problem is critical in the Motion History Image (MHI) method and we will redefine and explain in more details in later chapter.
- Actions are taken in flat plane, not in hilly part or stairs or uphill or downhill. For example, walking up to an uphill or downhill will provide different representations than walking in a flat plane. So far, most of the actions are considered in a place having flat or almost plain planes. It is however important to consider these cases.
- Almost in every method, the action patterns or directions are within a limited set of classes. For some methods, walking from right direction becomes different than walking from the left direction as those approaches cannot differentiate the walking action itself—they just differentiate some patterns of actions. Therefore, these approaches cannot be applicable to real-life scenarios.
- Actions' starting points and ending points are well-defined so that action classes can be easily isolated and managed.
- Movements are typically done in slower pace or at most in normal speed. Usually, we do not consider a mixed approach where a same action is done by various subjects in different paces. Also, the duration of an action is more or less similar in terms of number of frames. To elaborate this idea—let us assume that a person is running. Now, consider the scenarios of running as 100 m sprint race, 1,500 m, marathons of varied lengths and running by nonprofessionals from a slow to normal speeds. Now, many methods can not manage to recognize all sorts of running, as they cover varied speed, backgrounds, straight versus curved routes, etc. So, in simpler cases, actions are typically taken as slow or normal speed.
- In some simpler cases, one may consider to those actions that have only few moving limbs (e.g., waving hands, rotating an arm, kicking a ball, etc.). These are a few simplest possible action sets and easy to recognize.

These assumptions are considered based on applications and approaches. However, a new researcher may start with simpler cases with a number of assumptions and once the simpler cases are done, step-by-step, assumptions can be reduced and a more complex scenarios can be considered for analysis and recognition.

Fig. 1.3 Typical four basic steps up to recognition

1.3.4 Action Recognition: Some Basic Steps

There are a number of basic stages before having a recognized action class from a number of different actions. In this subsection, these will be explained, as shown in Fig. 1.3.

1.3.4.1 Preprocessing

To start with, a video is processed through some preprocessing steps. A video is considered as some series of consecutive image frames and each frame (based on the frame rate of that video) is processed and sequentially, the next frame is related to the previous frame(s). The preprocessing steps are mainly low-level image processing steps, e.g., filters are employed to reduce noises, edge detection, corner detection, feature extraction, smoothing or enhancing, normalization, etc.

Sometimes, some preconditions are met to start with processing an image of a scene. It is essential to start with some assumptions and with a correct interpretation of the present frame and move forward to the next frames based on some parameters. Calibrating camera is done in some applications. It is the process of finding the true camera parameters (that is represented in a 3×4 matrix, called *camera matrix*). The parameters are of two types:

- Intrinsic (or internal) parameters and
- Extrinsic parameters

There are five intrinsic parameters covering the focal length, image format, principal point (which would be in the center of the image in ideal case), skew parameter. External parameters for camera calibration covers rotation matrix and the position of origin of the world coordinate system expressed in coordinates of the camera-centric coordinate system.

Camera calibration (also called as camera resectioning) is a necessary step in 3D computer vision to extract metric information from 2D images, in augmented/virtual reality, reconstructing a world model, etc. [57]. Calibration techniques fall into mainly three broad categories: photogrammetric calibration, self-calibration, and other calibration techniques.

Photogrammetric calibration:

In this category, camera calibration is accomplished by observing a calibration object whose geometry in 3D space is known with very good precision [57]. The calibration object usually consists of two or three planes orthogonal to each other.

Sometimes, a plane undergoing a precisely known translation is also used [56]. These approaches require an expensive calibration apparatus, and an elaborate setup.

Self-calibration:

In self-calibration, as the name denotes—it does not need any calibration object [49]. It is flexible approach but not smarter compare to the photogrammetric calibration techniques. Just by moving a camera in a static scene, the rigidity of the scene provides in general two constraints on the cameras' internal parameters from one camera displacement by using image information alone [55, 57]. Therefore, if images are taken by the same camera with fixed internal parameters, correspondences among three images are sufficient to recover both the internal and external parameters [53, 54].

Other calibration techniques:

There are other approaches for camera calibration, as—vanishing points for orthogonal directions [51, 52], and calibration from pure rotation [50, 57].

In the cases of model-based action analysis and recognition, some prior information, e.g., kinematic structure (limb, skeleton), 3D shape, color appearance, pose, motion type, image patch, etc., are computed. Fully automatic initialization is one of the unsolved issues in this field.

1.3.4.2 Segmentation and Tracking Features

Through the employment of various methods of background subtraction, or frame to frame subtraction, or optical flow, or motion gradient, or streak-flow—segmentation of motion-centric regions are accomplished. However, each of these methods has varieties that will be suitable for specific scenarios. Segmented or extracted features from two consecutive frames are tracked in other frames, so that motion estimation or extraction can be accomplished. For the Motion History Image method, the segmentation or extraction of moving scenes can be done either through background subtraction or frame-to-frame subtraction method. However, the optical flow can be explored for the Motion History Image method.

1.3.4.3 Pose Estimation

Pose estimation is another basic step for action analysis and recognition though, in some cases, there is no demand for pose estimation specifically. For example, the Motion History Image method compute the motion information as cumulative motion *history* patterns and it ensures the poses where moving parts are involved. So, if an action has hand waving only, there will not be any clue on lower body part as no motion cues are present there. So, we do not need to process of estimating the configuration of the kinematic or skeletal articulation structure of a person for the MHI method.

Pose estimation may require geometric model or human model—either through the employment of body markers (which is essential for more accurate estimation in motion capture system) or without any body markers (where head and hands can be assumed as three points, and body center or mouth can be considered as a central/focal point of the subject's model). However, pose estimation without any body marker is difficult and too much erroneous—especially in the cases of partial occlusions due to body parts or motion overlapping. When we employ special markers to track the limbs, still there might have some missing markers due to occlusions. However, compared to no-marker situation, the presence of markers provide more robust estimation. For the case of MHI method, there is no need for body markers as it provides global motion information only.

There can be three different approaches on model:

- **Direct model**: Various model types are directly employed and the model is continuously updated by observations. In model-based recognition, researchers use information gathered from the human body, especially from the joints, to construct a model for recognition. In general, model-based approach is view and scale invariant [48]. Model types (e.g., stick figures, cylinders, patches, cones, rectangular, ellipse, box, etc.) are chosen empirically. Model parts are mainly considered from upper body or arms, legs, body, and head. Some of the model-based recognition systems require multicamera systems for collecting any information [48].

- **Indirect model**: Human model is indirectly used as a reference point or through a look-up table. The contents of a look-up table might be positions of body parts, aspect ratios of various limbs and so on. Of course, employment of indirect models are not sufficient but provide a supporting role for better pose analysis.

- **No model**: This is the model-free approach. Individual limbs or body parts are detected and then assembled through some simple manners (e.g., point-wise, simple shape or box, stick-figures, etc.) to estimate pose of a subject. Or model-free approaches exploit motion information directly without any need for a model reconstruction. Model-free approaches usually use sequences of binary silhouettes, extracting the silhouettes of moving objects from a video using segmentation techniques such as background subtraction [48].

1.3.4.4 Action Recognition

Action recognition is done finally! There can be three situations of visual abstractions, namely—

- Entire image can be assessed for analyzing and recognizing a scene. For example, in the case of any unusual event in crowd scene for any video surveillance system instead of extracting body parts of individual subject in the scene, the entire motion information in images can provide strong cue for any incidence.
- This is opposite to the above approach where a holistic recognition is done based on either the entire human body (as in the case of the MHI method) or some

body parts. Most of the silhouette-based or contour-based approaches fall in this category of action recognition.

- From entire image scene to entire human body—this final category recognizes some action primitives and grammars, based on semantic descriptions of body parts in smaller scales or objects. These are necessary for interpreting interactions or actions in a video, and understanding emotions.

1.3.5 Motion History Image

One of the most well-known methods for action representation and recognition is the Motion History Image method. In short, the Motion History Image approach is called the MHI image or MHI template or MHI method. In its basic format, the MHI is a temporal template that contains the *history* or *flow* of motion in a video sequence. The key attributes of the MHI are—

- It provides a simple representation of an action.
- It is a view-based approach.
- The MHI can demonstrate the flow of motion with some constraints.
- The MHI templates can be exploited for various applications—from recognition to action understanding.
- The computational cost of the MHI is minimal and hence, it can be useful for real-time applications.

This book will detail on the MHI representation and approaches related to the MHI method. We will present a detailed overview of this method in the next chapter. Readers may go through a shorter version on the MHI method from Ref. [700].

1.4 Conclusion

Understanding action is not the only thing that the vision community is looking for. Let us consider a service robot who will help a person in a rehabilitation center or hospital. Now, what that robot should have to know? Is it only understanding some actions or activities? Is it related to track one or more moving subjects? Is it related to recognizing various objects so that the service or nurse robot can help properly? In fact, the ability to recognize what parts of the whole task can be segmented and considered as subtasks so that it can perform online planning for task execution given the current state of the environment [35]. According to [35], some crucial problems related to this issue are,

- How should the robot be instructed that the temporal order of the subtasks may or may not matter?

- How should the scene, the objects and the changes that can be done to them be represented?
- Given a specific scene state, the robot may be unable to perform a particular action. For example, the representation may specify that water glasses can be piled on top of plates but robot may be unable to reach the desired height.
- The entire scene may change during the execution phase and the robot has to be able to react to sudden changes and replan its task.
- When there will be accident, e.g., on a slippery floor due to some water on the floor—then can it manage properly?

Therefore, these various aspects should be incorporated in the actual implementable planning for a robot. In reality, it is till date, far from this reality—mainly because, most of the action recognition analyses are concentrating on basic action sets and few activities. Moreover, the number of classes are limited too with constrained environment. We need to explore more!

Chapter 2
Action Representation

Abstract In this chapter, various action recognition issues are covered in a concise manner. Various approaches are presented here. In Chap. 1, nomenclatures, various aspects of action recognition are detailed. Hence, the previous chapter is crucial to provide a base for this chapter.

2.1 Action Recognition

Action recognition is a very important area in computer vision and other fields. We have different approaches for action recognition. These are defined based on the characteristics of different methods and their inherent strategies to deal with action classes. In one of the dominant classifications, action recognition approaches are divided into the following categories [505, 567]:

- Template matching approaches.
- State-space approaches.
- Semantic description of human behaviors.

Before presenting the Motion History Image method, we need to know the diversified approaches for action recognitions. Therefore, we devote this chapter to classify major approaches in various dimensions. We will notice that a number of approaches have been explored to solve the core problems of action recognition. Our concentration is mainly on the action *representations*—because without having smart and robust representations, it will not be possible to recognize actions in a reasonable manner. Though the pattern recognition part is significantly crucial for action recognition, this book does not deal much with machine learning methodologies. We feel that there are already a good amount of literatures in that arena.

Although it is a fact that researchers are investing enormous efforts to propose and justify their approaches for action or activity recognition—the reality is that this field is still not mature enough to be applicable in many important areas. As [558] reported earlier—the activity representation and recognition is relatively old,

Md. A. R. Ahad, *Motion History Images for Action Recognition and Understanding*, 19
SpringerBriefs in Computer Science, DOI: 10.1007/978-1-4471-4730-5_2,
© Md. Atiqur Rahman Ahad 2013

yet still immature! Different dimensions can be achieved from some survey papers on action recognition and related issues [494, 505, 506, 510, 539, 546–565, 700]. The following sections present different approaches for action recognition.

2.2 Approaches on Bag-of-Features

The bag-of-features approach [64] is a well-known method for action recognition. The *bag-of-features*-based approaches can be applied in classification by employing features as *words*. Due to its popularity, researchers are extensively considering this framework for their researches [148, 168, 440, 441, 446, 448, 449, 498, 601, 637, 638, 643, 646, 651, 652, 657]. It has similar versions in the literature as:

- Bag-of-Features [64, 168, 638, 652]
- Bag-of-Words [168]
- Bag-of-Visual-Words [168]
- Bag-of-Vocabularies [439]
- Bag-of-Video-Words [168]
- Bag-of-Points [697]

Now, what is the meaning of *bag* here as well as *words/features*? In fact, in order to represent an image template by considering the framework of bag-of-features or bag-of-words or similar—one can consider that image as a *document*, where *words* can be produced from the following steps:

- **Step-1—Feature detection:**
  This is one of the elementary image processing steps where image patches or points are analyzed to retrieve any significant image features. Now, what constitutes *features*? There is in fact no specific boundary or threshold to define a *feature* from an image template. A feature can be treated as the *interested points* for that specific image, which might not be *interesting* for another image or application. *Good features* are not defined and these are application-specific.

- **Step-2—Feature description or feature representation:**
  Once we have the image features—detected by one of the above-mentioned approaches, we can compute *numerical vectors* from these features. So, from an image—we extract features—then compute feature vectors by using an approach for feature description, called *feature descriptors*.

- **Step-3—Discrete vocabularies or dictionary or codebook generation:**
  From the above stage, we can have feature vectors from each image template. The feature vectors have equal dimensions for each image though the orders of different vectors have no importance. It is a constraint of bag-of-features. In the final stage, features are quantized into *discrete vocabularies* or *codewords* (similar to *words* in a *document*) and hence a *codebook* (similar to a *word dictionary*) are produced. These are clustered and hence a suitable clustering method should be selected. Therefore, we have a certain codeword that can relate to an image patch, and the image is represented by a histogram of the codewords.

The Bag-of-Features representation is typically a normalized histogram, where each bin in the histogram is the number of features assigned to a particular code divided by the total number of features in the video clip [709]. In short, a bag-of-words approach is as follows:

– Generates a vocabulary of visual words.
– Characterizes videos with the histograms of visual word counts.

In case of a video, we need to find a suitable approach to sample a video to extract localized features. Some approaches are [439]:

- Space-time interest point operators
- Grids/pyramids
- Random sampling

There are some clear-cut advantages of the bag-of-words framework, as [439]:

- It presents simple representation.
- It needs almost no preprocessing steps.

Some disadvantages of this framework are:

- We can notice in the steps of bag-of-features paradigm that the entire spatial arrangements of features are lost. This may be a major problem in some applications where relationships among various spatial arrangements are necessary. It is not possible to have an explicit model of a subject and hence, it cannot provide localized information.
- Another constraint is related to the missing spatio-temporal information. Thus, in case of any actions with several motion or posture changes (e.g., opening a door) and symmetric actions (e.g., 'sitting down' versus 'standing up' actions), this framework cannot perform well [150].
- In the recognition process, this framework cannot explicitly justify on where two actions are matching each other [439].
- If the codebook becomes very large, it may produce lower recognition. On the other hand, if the vocabulary size is small, it may cause over-clustering and poor recognition.
- The feature detection and vocabulary generation is time-taxing for large amount of data. Moreover, prior heavy training loads may deter the performance [632].
- Another constraint is related with the necessity of knowing the number of visual features, the size of vocabularies, the level of hierarchies, and the number of kernels for clustering, etc.

Some approaches to improve the performance of bag-of-words approaches: Due to its simplicity—the bag-of-features or bag-of-words frameworks get wide attention among researchers—not only for action recognition but also for object classification. Recently, a few approaches have been proposed to mitigate some of these constraints. For example, a bag-of-features method is proposed for learning discriminative features on space-time neighborhoods by [637], where the descriptors are modeled hierarchically and multiple kernel learning is used to characterize each action.

Usually, large vocabulary size of the bag-of-visual-words is more discriminative for inter-class action classification while a small one is more robust to noise and thus tolerant to the intra-class invariance [446]. In other words, it is common to choose an appropriately large vocabulary size. The larger the vocabulary size, the more chance to have a sparse histogram for each video, and thereby yield more noise and reduce the discriminability of vocabulary.

On the other side, if the vocabulary size is small, it may cause over-clustering and high intra-class distortion. In order to overcome this shortcoming, a pyramid vocabulary tree is proposed [446]. They cluster the interest points in the spatio-temporal space. The spatio-temporal space forms some cluster centers, where histograms of local features are produced. A sparse spatio-temporal pyramid matching kernel (SST-PMK) is proposed to compute the similarity measures between video sequences [446]. SST-PMK satisfies the Mercers condition and therefore is readily integrated into SVM to perform action recognition. They found that both the pyramid vocabulary tree and the SST-PMK lead to a significant improvement in human action recognition on the Weizmann dataset.

2.3 XYT: Space-Time Volume

Action recognition approaches can be based on space-time volume or spatio-temporal features. The *spatio* term is related to the *XY*/spatial domain and the *temporal* term is noting the *T*/time of an action. Let us consider an action in a video clip. We want to have its representation as a spatio-temporal template by combining the spatial motion information along with the temporal information. And from this template—if we can achieve significant motion information along its motion duration, then it will be very significant information for action recognition. This process is attempted to propose space-time volume-based methods for action recognition. One of the simplest but effective methods is the Motion History Image (MHI) method [492]. The MHI method itself consumes the temporal information in a template or final image from a video scene. Apart from the MHI method, a number of other methods have combined or incorporated the spatio-temporal information for better action representations.

Some key characteristics of the spatio-temporal features are:

- Space(X,Y)-time(T) descriptors may strongly depend on the relative motion between the object and camera.
- Some corner points in time, called space-time interest points, can automatically adapt the features to the local velocity of the image pattern.
- However, these space-time points are often found on highlights and shadows, hence, they are sensitive to lighting conditions and it may affect recognition accuracy.

Fig. 2.1 Example of spatio-temporal interest points (STIP) for an action

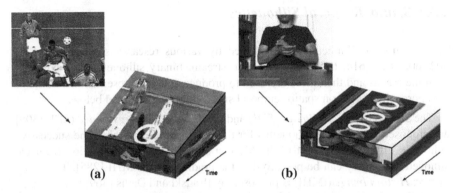

Fig. 2.2 Examples of detecting the strongest spatio-temporal interest points (STIP) **a** a football sequence with a player heading a ball; **b** a hand clapping sequence. With kind permission of Springer Science + Business Media B.V.—from Laptev [440]: Fig. 1, Springer, 2005

- Spatio-temporal features can avoid some limitations of traditional approaches of intensities, gradients, optical flow, and other local features.

Figure 2.1 depicts some spatio-temporal interest points for a walking action. Figure 2.2 shows some results of detecting the strongest spatio-temporal interest points in a football sequence with a player heading the ball and in a hand clapping sequence [440]. From these temporal slices of space-time volumes, it is evident that the detected events correspond to neighborhoods with high spatio-temporal variation in the image data.

Now we present a few methods that employ the spatio-temporal concepts to represent and extract motion information for recognition. References [600, 601] propose a volumetric *space-time action shapes* that are induced by a concatenation of 2D silhouettes in the space-time volume and contain both the spatial information about the posture of the human subject at any time (location and orientation of the torso and limbs, aspect ratio of different body parts), as well as the dynamic information (global body motion and motion of the limbs relative to the body) [601]. In the approach by [600], each internal point is assigned with the mean time required for a particle undergoing a random-walk process starting from the point to hit the boundaries. This method utilizes properties of the solution to the Poisson equation to extract space-time features such as local space-time saliency, action dynamics, shape structure, and orientation. These features are useful for action recognition, detection, and clustering [601]. In another similar approach, human actions are presented as 3D spatio-temporal surfaces and analyzed using differential geometric surface properties [608].

In Chap. 3, we present the MHI method and its variants in detail and most of the approaches are proposed with the concept of space-time volume, as these representations incorporate cumulative temporal information within the spatial domain.

2.3.1 Spatio-Temporal Silhouettes

Spatio-temporal silhouettes are exploited by various researches [483, 490, 531, 602, 608, 612, 614, 645]. From a video stream, binary silhouettes are extracted by some means and then these are used to produce action representations. Some of the approaches based on spatio-temporal silhouettes are presented below.

The *Silhouette History Image* (SHI) and the *Silhouette Energy Image* (SEI) [309] are proposed that exploit silhouettes for these two representations. The successive silhouette differences are set in the MHI in such a manner that motion from the silhouette boundary can be perceived in the gradient of the MHI [285]. The *timed Motion History Image* (tMHI) is proposed by Bradski and Davis [369] to generalize the MHI to directly encode time in a floating-point format. Another silhouette-based action modeling for recognition is presented by [324]. A probabilistic graphical model using ensembles of spatio-temporal patches is proposed by [614] in order to detect irregular behaviors in videos.

A number of gait recognition methods are based on spatio-temporal silhouettes. For example, the *Gait Energy Image* (GEI) [44, 297, 298], the *Frame Difference Energy Image* (FDEI) [42], the *Frame Difference History Image* (FDHI) [41], the *Average Motion Energy* (AME), the *Mean Motion Shape* (MMS) [612], the *Volume Motion Template* (VMT) [276, 502], the *Volumetric Motion History Image* (VMHI) [291, 328], the *Motion History Volume* (MHV) [531], and other methods [483, 490].

2.4 Interest-Point Detectors

Interest point detection is key to many methods for action recognition. For an image, finding the appropriate interest points and detecting those points or features are one part—while, for consecutive images from a video sequence, describing these points by feature descriptors is another dimension. One of the earliest but well-known and well-employed spatio-temporal feature or interest point detectors is the *Harris-Laplace detector* [440]. Which points or features are the key is difficult to decide [474]. Feature points can be considered based on corner points [440], the presence of global texture [473], periodicity [474], motion flow vectors [498], etc.

As defined above, from an image, features are extracted through some feature descriptors. Some of the important feature descriptors are:

- Scale-Invariant Feature Transform (SIFT).
- Rank Scale-Invariant Feature Transform.
- PCA-SIFT—It is a variant of SIFT.
- Generalized Robust Invariant Feature (G-RIF)—It considers edge density, edge orientation, etc., to produce a generalized robust feature descriptor as an extension of SIFT.
- Rotation-Invariant Feature Transform (RIFT)—It is a rotation-invariant version of SIFT, developed based on circular normalized patches.
- Speeded-Up Robust Feature (SURF), and its variants.
- Gradient Location and Orientation Histogram (GLOH)—It is a SIFT-like descriptor and it considers more spatial regions for the histograms. It is proposed to enhance robustness and distinctiveness of the SIFT.
- Local Energy-based Shape Histogram (LESH)—It is based on local energy model of features.
- Histogram of Oriented Gradients (HOG), and its variants.

The SURF (Speeded-Up Robust Features [399, 475]) is developed for interest point detection. The best feature descriptor should be invariant to rotation (RIFT), scale (e.g., SIFT, LESH), intensity, and affine variations to a significant level. However, none of the above descriptors are invariant to rotation, scale, intensity, and affine changes in a smart manner. Among these, the Scale-Invariant Feature Transform (SIFT) performs well. Now, regarding the computation of *feature descriptor* as numerical vectors, the SIFT can convert an image patch into 128-dimensional vector, SURF can produce 64-dimensional vector (in order to reduce the time for feature computation); PCA-SIFT reduces to 36-dimensions with PCA, GLOH estimates a vector having 128- or 64-dimensions.

There are numerous ways to detect features [477, 618] (e.g., edges, corners, patches, interest points, blobs or region of interest (ROI), ridges, etc.) from an image, such as:

- *Edge detection*
  - Canny edge detection
  - Sobel operator
  - Prewitt filter
  - Roberts Cross
  - Canny-Deriche
  - Differential edge detection

  – Hough transforms
  – Harris and Stephens / Plessey
  – Smallest Univalue Segment Assimilating Nucleus (SUSAN)

- *Blob detection*

  – Laplacian of Gaussian (LoG)
  – Difference of Gaussian (DoG)
  – Determinant of Hessian (DoH)
  – Principal Curvature-based Region Detector (PCBR)
  – Hessian-affine
  – Hessian-Laplace
  – Harris-affine
  – Maximally Stable extremal Regions (MSER)
  – Lindeberg's Watershed-based Gray-level Blob detector

- *Corner detection*

  – Multi-scale Harris operator
  – Harris and Stephens algorithm
  – Level curve curvature approach
  – Affine-adapted interest point operators
  – SUSAN corner detector
  – Wang and Bradly corner detector
  – Accelerated Segment Test (AST)-based feature detector
  – Features from Accelerated Segment Test (FAST)
  – Shi and Tomasi
  – LoG
  – DoG
  – DoH
  – Moravec algorithm
  – Foerstner corner detector

- *Hough transform, Kernel-based Hough transform*
- *Structure tensor*
- *Ridge detector*

These are based on whether regions of the image or the blob or corner should be detected as key interest points. Usually, it is beneficial to exploit spatio-temporal features due to the fact that it may overcome the constraints related to the computation of optical flow, feature tracking, selection of key frames, extraction of silhouettes, etc. [486, 598, 599, 601]. The optical flow is noisy and it faces aperture problems, smooth surfaces, singularities, etc. Feature tracking has the problem of occlusions, self-occlusions, re-initialization, and change of appearance. Interest points can be considered as the salient points or regions. Approaches that deal with these issues are [601, 602, 605, 607, 608, 638, 643, 649, 651, 653, 654].

The following descriptors can encode the spatio-temporal support region of these interest points, according to [36]:

- Histograms of Oriented Gradient (HOG) descriptor
- SIFT and SURF descriptors
- Histograms of Optic Flow (HOF) descriptor
- Point-trajectory features
- Vector of concatenated pixel gradients
- Local jet descriptors
- Volumetric features

Reference [282] propose the *Histograms of Oriented Gradient* (HOG) descriptor [63, 66, 148, 282, 638, 698] for human detection and recognition. The *Histograms of Optic Flow* (HOF) descriptors [63, 148, 638] are proposed based on optical flow. Performances and popularities of the HOF descriptor are less than the HOG descriptors. The generalized SURF and SIFT descriptors are also popular [592, 635, 656, 658]. On the contrary, the descriptors based on point-trajectory features [65, 148], pixel gradients [652], local jet [651] and volumetric features [148, 531] are emerging descriptors and hence, detailed information about their performances and constraints are not sufficient. However, the volumetric features can be useful in view-invariant action recognition.

2.5 Local Discriminative Approaches

In different domains, action recognition is accomplished by:

- Action recognition based on large-scale features.
- Action recognition based on local patches.
- Action recognition based on mixed or mid-level approach of the above two methodologies.

2.5.1 Large-Scale Features-Based Recognition

One of the large-scale features is optical flow-based approach. It is used as a spatio-temporal descriptor for action recognition [182, 493]. Large-scale feature describes the entire human figure. Reference [493] recognizes some actions at a distance where the resolution of each individual is small (e.g., about 30 pixels tall only). A motion descriptor is introduced where, the raw optical flow vector is split into four different channels. Initially, the optical flow vector field is split into two scalar fields corresponding to the horizontal and vertical components of the flow, F_x and F_y, each of which is then half-wave rectified into four non-negative channels [493]. These are called spatio-temporal motion descriptors, which can be considered as large-scale features, encompassing the entire image. They classify three datasets: ballet dataset, real tennis data from a static camera, and soccer game from moving camera.

2.5.2 *Local Patches-Based Recognition*

Reference [613] classifies spatial histogram feature vectors into prototypes. Local patches mean part-based models for action representation. Local features describe small patches. Though conceptually appealing and promising—the merit of part-based models has not yet been widely recognized in action recognition [182]. A bag-of-words representation can be used to model these local patches for action recognition. One of the key concerns of this approach is that it suffers from the same restriction of conditional independence assumption that ignores the spatial structure of the parts.

2.5.3 *Mixed Approach for Recognition*

This hybrid approach combines the large-scale features with local patches for better recognition [27, 182, 452]. Reference [182] introduces a similar concept where a human action is represented by the combination of large-scale global features and local patch features. Reference [452] presents a method of recognition that learns mid-level motion features. In another approach, optical flow is used as large-scale features and SURF is used, where extracted SURF descriptors represent local appearances around interest points [27].

If the complexity of actions increases, the recognition methods become more difficult. Therefore, use of a combination of feature types is necessary. For example, with the *Coffee and Cigarettes Dataset*, which is a difficult dataset, a combination of feature types is considered by [659].

2.6 View-Invariant Approaches

View-invariant methods are difficult and hence, most of the methods are view-variant instead of being view-invariant. The Motion History Image method is basically a view-based method. We will see in a later chapter that some approaches have been proposed to convert the MHI from view-based to view-invariant method, namely the Motion History Volumes (MHV), Volume Motion Templates (VMT), 3D-MHI, etc.

It is very difficult to develop a system that is fully view-invariant due to various reasons [36], such as:

- Occlusion due to object, body parts, motion self-occlusion.
- Similar actions seen from different angles may appear as different actions.
- Multi-camera coordination and management.
- Computational cost.

A number of view-invariant methods are available in [21, 22, 24–26, 276, 277, 279, 280, 291, 308, 328, 420, 421, 502, 503, 509, 511, 531, 583, 590, 593, 594]. Most of the view-invariant methods exploit video streams from multiple-camera from different angles. INRIA IXMAS action dataset is one of the widely used datasets for this purpose. In a few cases, stereo cameras, Kinect sensor (which has stereo camera too) are used [26, 502].

Each action is represented as a unique curve in a 3D invariance-space, surrounded by an acceptance volume called *action-volume*. It is proposed by [23]. Reference [24] proposes a *Spatio-Temporal Manifold* (STM) model to analyze nonlinear multivariate time series with latent spatial structure and applies it to recognize actions in the joint-trajectories space. It is a view-invariant approach. Reference [25] presents a two-layer classification model for view-invariant human action recognition based on interest points. In this work, training videos of every action are recorded from multiple viewpoints and represented as space-time interest points.

Reference [22] presents a framework for learning a compact representation of primitive actions (e.g., walk, punch, kick, sit) that can be used for video obtained from a single camera for simultaneous action recognition and viewpoint estimation. Reference [21] introduces the idea that the motion of an articulated body can be decomposed into rigid motions of planes defined by triplets of body points.

Some view-invariant methods of the 2D Motion History Image (MHI) representation are proposed and these are detailed in Chap. 3. For example, the *Volume Motion Template* (VMT) is proposed as view-invariant 3D action recognition method [502] and they use only a stereo-camera to produce their results in a view-invariance manner. Weinland et al. [279, 503, 531] introduce the *Motion History Volume* (MHV) method—a view-invariant approach with the concept of the 2D MHI. Reference [303] proposes the *3D Motion History Model* (3D-MHM) as a view-invariant MHI. In a similar fashion, [280, 509] incorporate the information of position of body limbs, and develop a method called *Motion History Volume* (MHV) as a 3D-MHI and *Motion Energy Volume* (MEV) as a 3D-MEI template. Another 3D-MHI representation, called the *Volumetric Motion History Image* (VMHI) is proposed by [291, 328].

In another dimension, [26] presents a novel approach for human action recognition with *Histograms of 3D Joint* locations (HOJ3D) as a compact representation of postures. They extract the 3D skeletal joint locations from depth maps from Kinect sensor by using Shotton's method. As the Kinect sensor is an important addition that provides depth images along with color images—in future, we will see more approaches that lead us to better view-invariant methods.

2.7 Conclusion

In this chapter, we present important divisions and varieties of action recognition strategies. As the book is about the Motion History Image (MHI)—we do not have enough scope to detail other methods. These glimpses provide a foundation on dimensions of action recognition. In Chap. 3, we present the MHI method and its representations in detail.

Chapter 3
Motion History Image

Abstract This chapter presents the Motion History Image (MHI) and the Motion Energy Image (MEI) templates, which have been in use by researchers for over a decade due to its simplicity and ease to implement with good performance. A tutorial on the MHI method is presented here. It covers the shortcomings of the MHI methods and presents various developed methods at the top of the MHI—both in 2D and in 3D. To our knowledge and till-to-date, this is the most comprehensive and detailed presentation on the MHI method/representation.

3.1 Motion History Image and its Importance

This chapter is about the Motion History Image (MHI) method. The MHI method is, in fact, a smart action representation approach. When the concept of the MHI is proposed during 1996/1997, the Motion History Image is explained and presented as a new concept by which moving parts of a video sequence can be engraved in a single image, from where one can predict the motion flow as well as the moving parts of the video action. Later this action/motion representation approach becomes very popular due to its simple algorithm and easy to implement. Afterwards, Bobick and Davis employed this MHI together with another related representation called the Motion Energy Image (MEI) for classifying some aerobics. Since then, the MHI/MEI representations for various applications, or the MHI method (that combines the MEI in most of the cases) for action recognition become very popular in the computer vision community.

Some important features of the MHI representation are mentioned below:

- The MHI can represent motion sequence in a compact manner. In this case, the silhouette sequence is condensed into gray scale image, where dominant motion information is preserved.
- Due to its inherent algorithm, the MHI can be created and implemented in low illumination conditions where structure cannot be easily detected otherwise. For example, in surveillance applications, it is very effective [308].

Md. A. R. Ahad, *Motion History Images for Action Recognition and Understanding*, 31
SpringerBriefs in Computer Science, DOI: 10.1007/978-1-4471-4730-5_3,
© Md. Atiqur Rahman Ahad 2013

- The MHI representation is not so sensitive to silhouette noises, holes, shadows, and missing parts [330]. However, if there is a significant presence of shadow in the moving scene, the MHI will also incorporate significant shadow information.
- The gray-scale MHI is sensitive to the direction of motion because it can demonstrate the flow direction of the motion. That's why it is better-suited for discriminating between actions of opposite directions. For example, a *running* action in left direction is different than the same in right direction [332]—though for some approaches, it might be problematic, as the action itself is *running*, only the directions are different.
- It keeps a history of temporal changes at each pixel location, which then decays over time [331].
- As the MHI representation recognizes general patterns of movement, it can be implemented with cheap cameras and normal processors [369].
- The MHI expresses the motion flow or sequence by using the intensity of every pixel in temporal manner. The MHI representation can encode a range of times in a final and one frame [369].

3.1.1 Applications of the MHI Method/Representation

The Motion History Image representation is considered in many applications related to action recognition and video analysis. We notice that along with the MHI, the Motion Energy Image (MEI) is also employed for better results. The following parts in this subsection will present the important applications based on the MHI and/or MEI method or representation. Here, we group the applications into the following subdivisions,

- Action recognition
- Gesture recognition
- Gait recognition
- Video analysis

3.1.1.1 Action Recognition with the MHI

The main application area of the Motion History Image (MHI) method is to recognize various actions. These are view-based and template-based action recognition approaches, except a few developments on 3D-based MHI for view-invariance recognition. Here, we present action recognition strategies taken by various groups in different datasets [267, 277, 279, 280, 292, 304, 309, 310, 315–317, 323, 324, 327, 374, 492, 503, 509, 526, 531, 542, 543, 612, 700]. We notice that most of these recognition trials are accomplished with personal or less well-known datasets [266, 601, 651].

- In the original paper on the MHI method [492], good recognition results are achieved. From the MHI templates, Hu moments are computed for each action as feature vector. Employing the Mahalanobis distance with 18 aerobics by one expert instructor, with repetitions, from multi-camera setting, the MHI method is proposed for action recognition.

- Naiel et al. [39] employ the MHI/MEI with *2-Dimensional Principal Component Analysis* (2DPCA) and recognize various actions from Weizmann dataset and INRIA IXMAS dataset. The 2DPCA is more efficient in terms of storage requirements and computational complexity compared to the conventional PCA. With the Weizmann dataset, 98.89 % recognition result is achieved with this approach. On the other hand, with the INRIA IXMAS multi-view dataset, an average accuracy of 84.59 % is achieved.
- Reference [327] employ the MHI, MEI, and Local Binary Pattern (LBP) with the Hidden Markov Model to recognize 10 actions from 9 subjects, and they achieve 97.8 % recognition rate.
- Reference [292] use the MHI and *Fisher Discriminant Analysis* (FDA), to recognize 4 actions (i.e., jumping, squatting, limping, and walking) by 20 subjects, and they achieve 90 % recognition result. Figure 3.1 shows Motion History Images (MHI) of events—flapping, squatting, and waving, respectively. The MHI features computed using four actions of events—*click* and *no*—are shown here. Their corresponding discriminatory potentials are 0.006, 0.030, 0.152, and 0.197. The first two actions have low discriminatory potential owing to their similarity. The last two actions are more useful for the classification task [292].
- Reference [315] propose the *Action Energy Image* (AEI) and use eigen decomposition of an AEI in eigen activity space obtained by PCA, which best represents the AEI data in least-square sense. They use *Gaussian Mixture Model* (GMM) background model for background subtraction. They achieve 93.8 % recognition results in the Weizmann dataset having 9 actions from 9 subjects [601].
- Reference [304] develop a method called *Motion Energy Histogram* (MEH), which is a histogram-based approach to improve the computation efficiency. To utilize the multi-resolution structure more efficiently, they propose an automated uneven partitioning method which is achieved by utilizing the quad-tree decomposition results of the MEH. They employ their method in Weizmann dataset [601] (instead of covering all actions, they consider 7 actions only from 9 subjects). However, they add additional 10 subjects with their own videos in a different environment to enlarge the database. They achieve 98.5 % recognition rate.
- Reference [612] propose *Average Motion Energy* (AME) and *Mean Motion Shape* (MSS). For recognition, the K-nearest neighbor (KNN) and NN approach is taken. They employ 10 activities from 9 subjects [601] and achieve about 100 % recognition result.
- Reference [710] propose a new approach called implicit Motion-shape Model based on the MHI images for action recognition. They divide the MHI into local *Motion-Shape* regions, which allows to analyze the action as a set of sparse space-time patches in 3D. With the KTH and Weizmann dataset, they achieve good results.
- Figure 3.2 demonstrates few MHI [492] and modified-MHI images [305] based on six actions taken from KTH dataset [651].

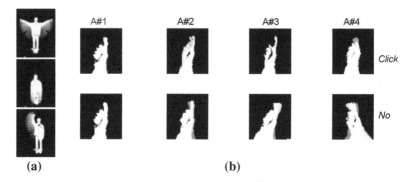

(a)   (b)

Fig. 3.1 **a** MHI images for three events. **b** MHI features computed using four actions of the events *Click* and *No*. With kind permission from Springer Science+Business Media B.V.—from Alahari and Jawahar [292], Fig. 3, Springer, 2006

Fig. 3.2 Examples of the MHI and modified-MHI for six actions from KTH dataset: *Top-row* for action frames; *mid-row* depicts the corresponding MHI images; and *bottom-row* shows the modified-MHI. With kind permission from Springer Science+Business Media B.V.—from Meng et al. [318]

It is found that for the KTH dataset, the average recognition rates are about 63.5, 61.5, and 65.25 % using the MHI [492], the modified-MHI [305] and the combined features of the MHI and the modified-MHI [318], respectively.

- On the other hand, Ref. [309] propose *Silhouette History Image* (SHI) and *Silhouette Energy Image* (SEI) to represent actions. Then Hu moment and Zernike moment are computed as feature vector. By using the KTH dataset of 6 actions from 25 subjects [651], the achieved recognition result is 87.5 %.

- Meng et al. [317] introduce a new motion representation called the *Hierarchical Motion History Histogram* (HMHH). With the MHI and HMHH as action representations, the *Support Vector Machine* (SVM) is run for recognition by considering the KTH dataset of 6 actions from 25 subjects [651]. The recognition result is not comparable with the state-of-the-art and they achieve 80.3 % recognition rate.

- Ahad et al. [542, 543] propose the *Directional Motion History Image* (DMHI) method. They compare the DMHI with MHI, HMHH, and *Multi-level MHI* (MMHI) methods for 10 aerobics from 8 subjects. For the DMHI, the recognition result is optimum and 94 % recognition rate. Moreover, [267] consider another dataset of 5 actions from 9 subjects from multi-camera and the achieved recognition result is 93 %.

- Reference [374] incorporate the Fourier and *Dynamic Time Warping* (DTW) with the MHI images to recognize 7 videos by 6 subjects. They achieve 85.5 % recognition results. In INRIA IXMAS action dataset [266], their achieved result is better and 87 %.
- Reference [324] compute the MHI images. These MHI images are projected into a new subspace by means of the Kohonen Self Organizing feature Map (SOM) and actions are recognized by Maximum Likelihood (ML) classifier in INRIA IXMAS action dataset [266]. In this approach, the recognition result is 77.27 %. They also run their approach in VIHASI database of 20 actions from 9 actors [120] with 98.5 % recognition result.
- Reference [310] use the MHI with *Higher order Local Autocorrelation* (HLAC) features and *Principal Component Analysis* (PCA). Using some actions of pitching of baseball, they achieve good recognition results (i.e., 100 % with 90 × 90 image resolution and 96.7 % with 25 × 25 image resolution). However, these actions are simple.
- Reference [277] present a multi-level sequential reliable inference method. They compute Hu moments from the MHI template and employ Expectation Maximization (EM) algorithm and Bayesian Information Criterion (BIC). In their experiments, three actions (walking, running, and standing at different styles) by 3 subjects in 8 different viewpoints are considered and in this difficult situation, the recognition result is 77 %. Actions are recorded by using a FLIR (thermal) video surveillance camera.
- One of the earliest works on the MHI concept [526] exploit the MHI templates with the Hu moments as feature vectors. PCA is employed for feature reduction and K-nearest neighbor classifier is used to classify 8 actions from 7 subjects. This approach shows reasonable recognition results.
- In another approach by [323], the MHI templates are used and various pattern recognition strategies are used like the k-nearest neighbor, neural network, Support Vector Machine (SVM), and Bayes Classifier. Their action database consists of 7 actions from 5 subjects, with repetitions. The achieved recognition result is 98 %.
- Canton et al. [280, 509] propose a 3D-MHI model, where feature vectors are calculated from 3D moment. PCA is used for reducing feature vectors. For their experiments, 8 actions are considered from 5 calibrated wide-lens cameras and they achieve 98 % recognition rate.
- Weinland et al. [279, 503, 531] develop another 3D-MHI model where they exploit the *Linear Discriminant Analysis* (LDA) and Mahalanobis distance for pattern recognition. They achieve 93.3 % recognition result in INRIA IXMAS Action dataset [266].
- Reference [316] introduce a modified version of the MHI called EMHI. With the PCA and SVM for classification, this approach performs poorly (recognition rate is only 63 %) for six simple actions.

- Reference [711] propose a Hierarchical Filtered Motion (HFM) method to recognize actions in crowded videos by using Motion History Image (MHI) as basic representations of motion due to its robustness and efficiency. In this method, interest points are detected as 2D Harris corners with recent motion (e.g., locations with high intensities in MHI). Histograms of Oriented Gradients (HOG) is used and Gaussian Mixture Model (GMM)-based classifier is exploited to recognize cross dataset of KTH and MSR Action Dataset II. They achieved good recognition results with difficult scenarios in presence of multiple persons.

3.1.1.2 Gesture Recognition with the MHI

The Motion History Image (MHI) can be directly employed for gesture recognition. Though there are some modifications on the basic MHI formation, these various representations are also simple to develop and hence, produce good recognition results. Apart from the similarities in representations—these approaches differ a lot in terms of the analysis of feature vectors and their productions, as well as classification methods [270, 271, 274, 292, 307, 314, 326, 327, 362, 374, 502]. In the following points, applications on gesture recognition are presented,

- References [314, 362] consider the Silhouette History and Energy images as SHI and SEI. Feature vectors are computed based on Hu moment and Zernike moment. With the Korean Gesture dataset having 14 actions from 20 subjects [262], their achieved recognition rate is 89.4 %.
- Reference [276] consider global gradient orientation and with only four gestures from stereo camera, they achieve 90 % recognition rate.
- Reference [274] exploit the MHI representation for PDA-based gesture recognition.
- Reference [292] use the MHI with the Fisher Discriminant Analysis (FDA). Hand gesture videos from Marcel's Dynamic Hand Gesture database [46] are used. It consists of 15 video sequences for each of the 4 dynamic hand gestures, namely Click, No, StopGraspOk and Rotate.
- With the combination of the MHI, Fourier transform and Dynamic Time Warping (DTW), [374] achieve 92 % recognition result on a dataset that has 14 gestures by 5 subjects, with repetitions.
- Reference [271] use the MHI to recognize 10 gestures from stereo camera and the result is promising with 90 % recognition.
- Combination of the *Motion Color Image* (MCI), the MHI, and the MEI provide 90 % recognition for 11 simple gestures [307].
- Reference [327] use the MHI and MEI. The *Local Binary Pattern* (LBP) is extracted and Hidden Markov Model is employed for 15 gestures from 5 subjects [263] to have 95 % recognition.
- The *Volume Motion Template* (VMT) is proposed as view-invariant 3D action recognition system [502]. With 10 gestures from 7 viewpoints, with repetitions, 90 % recognition result is achieved.

- The MHI is exploited where Hu moments are used as feature vectors and *Artificial Neural Network* (ANN) is used for classification [270]. Using 5 gestures from 5 subjects, having repetitions—96 % recognition result is achieved.
- Several gestures are recognized by a robot by considering the MHI, Hu moment, Mean-shift tracker, Particle Filter, and Mahalanobis distance [326].
- The MHI is used for extracting the moving information for sign language recognition system for mobile use [712]. As the MHI images tend to amplify the motion at the boundaries of an object and produce sharp steps, one can not consider these images directly for sign language application. Therefore, they reduce the sharp steps by convolving each MHI image with a Gaussian kernel, where the intensity level can be regarded as probability for motion.

3.1.1.3 Gait Recognition with the MHI

A number of gait recognition approaches are presented with the MHI representation as well as, with some modified versions of the MHI representations [297–304, 361]. Some of these approaches use benchmark datasets, e.g., CASIA Gait Database (A)/(B) [264], CMU Mobo Gait Database, and USF HumanID Gait Database [265]. These are mentioned below:

- A clustered-based *Dominant Energy Image* (DEI) is proposed by [302] where the frieze and wavelet features are used for feature vectors, and *Hidden Markov Model* (HMM) is employed for recognition. They use CASIA Gait Database (B) [264] with 93.9 % recognition rate. They also exploit the CMU Mobo Gait Database at 82 % recognition accuracy.
- The *Motion Energy Histogram* (MEH) is proposed and with the quad-tree structure, 96.4 % recognition is achieved in CASIA Gait Database (B) [264].
- The *Gait Energy Image* (GEI) [299, 300] is used for gait analysis and with the CASIA gait database [264], 90.5 % recognition rate is achieved.
- References [297, 298, 361] use the PCA and *Multiple Discriminant Analysis* (MDA), and with the USF HumanID Gait Database [265], 71 % recognition result is achieved.
- The *Gait Energy Image* (GEI) [301] and Gabor filter is used to recognize gait from the USF HumanID Gait Database [265] and they achieve slightly better recognition result than [297, 298, 361].
- The *Gait Moment Energy* (GMI) and the *Moment Deviation Image* (MDI) are introduced by [303]. With the K-nearest neighbor classifier in USF HumanID Gait Database [265], they notice only 66 % recognition rate.

3.1.1.4 Video Analysis Using the MHI

Apart from action, gesture, and gait recognition—the Motion History Image representations are used for various video analysis, tracking, behavior analysis, and so on by [269, 273, 281, 291, 295, 306, 308, 322, 328, 360, 507, 512, 513, 523, 528, 530, 532–534, 542, 694]:

- Video shot classification is done by considering *Edge Motion History Image* (EMHI) [311, 316]. They choose 60 minutes CNN video from the TRECVID'05 dataset to estimate all the GMMs in layer 1 and layer 2. Classification topics of video shots are based on the TRECVID'03 dataset, where randomly extracted 100 video shots are considered. Six different classes: indoor, outdoor, news-person, news-subject, sport, and weather are tested [316].

- Moving object is detected and localized under realistic conditions based on the MHI representation by [523, 534]. They incorporate the timed-Motion History Image for motion trajectory representation. Afterwards, a spatio-temporal segmentation procedure is employed to label motion regions by estimating density gradient in the spatio-temporal domain.

- A video surveillance system using Pan/Tilt/Zoom (PTZ) cameras is developed by [308] where an adaptive camera navigation model is constructed that can learn and locate activity regions of interest based on the concept of the MHI representation. From each PTZ camera, to find activity regions, MHI images are extracted from each scene. Then each blob of the moving scenes are analyzed to determine whether a blob is a potential candidate (i.e., translating motion) for human activity or not. The experiments are conducted for outdoor real-life scenes.

- Tracking of moving objects is done by using the MHI [269, 360]. Reference [360] assume that their system observes multiple moving objects via a single, uncalibrated video camera. A trajectory-guided recognition (TGR) approach is proposed as an efficient method for adaptive classification of action. The TGR approach is defined by the Motion History Images that are then recognized via a mixture of Gaussian classifier.

Basic steps for [360]:
Low-level image processing ⇒ Tracking ⇒ 3D trajectory recovery ⇒ Occlusion reasoning ⇒ Motion recognition

- Action line rendering is done by [295]. The author proposes a system for *line fitter*—a system for fitting lines to a video sequence that describes its motion. After the generation of the MHI, a line scoring scheme is implemented. This score is based upon the MHI pixel values that the line passes through. By plotting these values as a function of position on the line, projections of image onto the line can be produced.

Basic steps are [295]:
Line model ⇒ MHI generation ⇒ Line scoring ⇒ Candidate generation ⇒ Candidate subset selection ⇒ Action line fitting

- Petras et al. [281] use the *Motion History Volume* (MHV) [280, 509]—a 3D representation of the 2D-MHI—for detecting unusual behavior for video surveillance. The experimentations are taken in outdoor and in real-life situations.

- Albu et al. [291, 328] develop systems for the analysis of irregularities in human action and to detect unusual behavior. They employ a 3D-MHI model, called the *Volumetric Motion History Image* (VMHI), for five different actions. Their approach is found to be invariant to motion self-occlusion, speed variability in action, and in variable-length motion sequences.
- Son et al. [528] calculate the MHI and then combine with a background model to detect the candidate road image.
- Jin et al. [306] segment human body and measure its motion by employing the MHI.
- A motion segmentation method is developed by [542] by computing the optical flow and split the flow vectors into four different channels. The experiments are done both in indoor and outdoor environment.
- Albu et al. [291] analyze irregularities in human actions by MHI model.
- A perceptually-based, interactive, and narrative play space for children is developed and demonstrated by [507], called KidsRoom. Images, music, narration, light, and sound effects are used to transform a normal child's bedroom into a fantasy land where children are guided through a reactive adventure story. It is the first multi-person, fully-automated, interactive, and narrative environment ever constructed using non-encumbering sensors [507].

Basic steps are:
MHI generation ⇒ Object tracking ⇒ Movement detection ⇒ Action recognition in the Monster World:
General dynamics based on blob ⇒ Pose recognition ⇒ Movement recognition ⇒ Event detection ⇒ Interactions

In addition to the perceptual input technology, the KidsRoom has a narrative control program, a lighting control program, MIDI music control programs, and networking protocols [507].

- Davis et al. [513] develop a *virtual aerobics trainer* that watches and responds to the user as he/she performs the workout.
- For interactive arts, motion swarm is demonstrated by [694].
- Another interactive arts system is demonstrated by [512].
- Valstar et al. [273, 530] and Pantic et al. [322] detect few facial action units (AU).
- Yau et al. [532, 533] develop a strategy by the MHI representation for visual speech recognition.
- Similar to the concept of the MHI, [713] compute MHI and MEI for tracking people in dynamic and charging environments from camera mounted on a mobile robot.
- Another application in parking lots to look for any suspicious acts that lead to motor vehicle break-ins and/or theft is experimented by Brown et al. [714]. They exploit the MHI to detect any suspicious activity. In their implementation of the MHI, four frames from the frame differencing phase are combined to produce the MHI.
- Another approach for detecting temporal activity or activity area of a video has exploited the MEI and MHI separately [715].

3.2 Motion History Image: A Tutorial

In this section, a tutorial on the Motion History Image method is presented. As per the basic format by [492], we start with the construction of a binary Motion Energy Image (MEI). The MEI is an image that represents *where* motion has occurred in an image sequence [492]. Afterwards, the construction of the Motion History Image (MHI) is presented. These two representations—the MHI and the MEI together form a *temporal template*, which is a vector-valued image where each component of each pixel is some functions of the motion at that pixel location. These view-specific templates are matched against the stored models of views of known movements [492]. When these two representations or templates are considered for recognition by employing classification methods—it is called the MHI method for action or activity or gesture or gait recognition. The MHI and the MEI are two vector images that can encode a variety of motion properties within the final templates of the MHI and the MEI.

3.2.1 Construction of the Motion Energy Image (MEI)

We start with the Motion Energy Image (MEI) that encompasses the motion-occurring regions of a video scene. The MEI is a binary image, where the *white* region represents the motion occurring region and the *black* region denotes non-moving region. Initially, the MEI is also mentioned as *Binary Motion Region* (BMR) by [333]. The Motion Energy Image (MEI) is defined based on the spatial motion pattern of a scene as a binary image. The MEI represents an image—where motion has occurred [332, 492] in a video scene.

If two consecutive images have some changes in it, i.e., have some presence of motion—then the constructed MEI image will have pixel values of '1' for those pixels where some changes are present. Similarly, if the next image has any pixel changes or moving portion, then the additional pixels will be changed from '0' to '1'. Through this manner, a cumulative binary image is developed that presents the history of the motion presence as a binary image. The white pixels—having pixel value '1' can be noted as the *energy* of that image. Some of the key features of the Motion Energy Image are pointed below:

- The MEI provides only the regions—*where* motion or moving scenes were present. We will soon notice that the MHI, on the other hand, demonstrates *how*—instead of *where* only—the movement occurred or in which directions and intensity.
- From MEI, we can easily visualize the video sequence where it sweeps out a particular region of the image.
- It can determine subtly about the shape of the moving regions in that video. However, sometimes due to any presence of noise, an MEI image might show some parts, which should not be considered as moving regions.

- In short, the MEI is an image that suggests the movement occurring region(s) [334].
- A binary MEI is initially computed to act as an index into the action library. This coarsely describes the spatial distribution of motion energy for a given view of a given action. Any stored MEIs that plausibly match the unknown input MEI are then tested for a coarse, motion history agreement with a known motion model of the action [741].

According to [492], let us consider that $I(x, y, t)$ be an image sequence, and let $D(x, y, t)$ be a binary image sequence that indicates the regions of moving scenes in a video sequence. It can be done by employing a background subtraction method if a prior background is available, or if a background model can be developed on the fly. Other well-known options are frame subtraction approach, or optical flow method, etc. $D(x, y, t)$ is generated by one of these approaches. Then, the binary Motion Energy Image (MEI) $E_\tau(x, y, t)$ can be defined by,

$$E_\tau(x, y, t) = \bigcup_{i=0}^{\tau-1} D(x, y, t - i) \tag{3.1}$$

In the above equation, the critical parameter is the selection of the τ. It is critical in defining the temporal extent of a movement [492]. If the value of τ is very large, all the differences are accumulated in the MEI. The τ has a vast influence on the temporal representation of a movement. Later, we will show how an MEI image can be retrieved from an MHI image.

3.2.2 Construction of the Motion History Image (MHI)

In this subsection, we will explain the construction of the Motion History Image. Intensity of each pixel in the MHI is a function of motion density at that location. From the MHI image, we can notice that newer movement is brighter. Let's consider that two neighboring or consecutive images can be described by,

$$I(x, y, t) = b_t(x, y) + m_t(x, y) + n_t(x, y)$$
$$I(x, y, t + 1) = b_{t+1}(x, y) + m_{t+1}(x, y) + n_{t+1}(x, y) \tag{3.2}$$

where,
$b_t(x, y)$: Static background for t_{th} frame.
$m_t(x, y)$: Moving objects for t_{th} frame.
$n_t(x, y)$: Background noise for t_{th} frame.

Now, if we consider consecutive frame differencing approach for extracting moving objects, we can get,

$$diff(x, y, t) = I(x, y, t+1) - I(x, y, t)$$
$$diff(x, y, t) = b(x, y) + md(x, y, t) + nd(x, y, t) \tag{3.3}$$

where,

$b(x, y, t)$: Overlapped area in consecutive frames.

$md(x, y, t)$: Motion region.

$nd(x, y, t)$: Noise (which can be ignored based on situations).

Note that $diff(x, y, t)$ contains part of moving object, background aberration due to motion and noise—that lead to incorrect results (e.g., over-segment, motion ambiguity, and distortion) and motion at low speed cannot be easily detected. To mitigate these constraints, one may convert this gray-scale image $diff(x, y, t)$ into binary image, $diff'(x, y, t)$. Therefore, let's define the $D(x, y, t)$ as,

$$D(x, y, t) = [D(x, y, t) * \tau]/255 \tag{3.4}$$

Then, by layering the successive $D(x, y, t)$, the Motion History Image can be produced. The MHI can be generated using difference of frames (DOF),

$$\Psi(x, y, t) = \begin{cases} 1 & \text{if } D(x, y, t) > \xi \\ 0 & \text{otherwise} \end{cases} \tag{3.5}$$

where, $\Psi(x, y, t)$ is the binarization of the difference of frames by considering a threshold ξ.

The parameter ξ is the minimal intensity difference between two images for change detection. The DOF of the t_{th} frame with difference distance Δ is,

$$D(x, y, t) = |I(x, y, t) - I(x, y, t \pm \Delta)| \tag{3.6}$$

Now, we can compute the MHI ($H_\tau(x, y, t)$) from the above update function ($\Psi(x, y, t)$) in a recursive manner,

$$H_\tau(x, y, t) = \begin{cases} \tau & \text{if } \Psi = 1 \\ \max(0, H_\tau(x, y, t-1) - 1) & \text{otherwise} \end{cases} \tag{3.7}$$

where,

(x, y): Pixel position.

t: Time that defines consecutive frames.

$\Psi(x, y, t)$: Update function that defines a presence of motion.

τ: Decides the temporal duration of the MHI.

In this manner, we can have a scalar-valued image (i.e., the MHI image) where more recently moving pixels are brighter. The above equation is based on [492] where pixel values are reduced by 1 (i.e., decay parameter is 1) if there is no more moving scene in that specific pixel value. For example, if $I(x, y, 2)$—the frame no.

2 has no moving scene and $I(x, y, 1)$ equals $I(x, y, 2)$—then the produced MHI will be 100 % black or all pixel values will be zero. Now, if $I(x, y, 3)$ has a moving part at pixel (2,3), (3,3), and (3,4)—then those pixel values (which are zero till now) will be replaced by the value of τ (which can be the no. of video frames in that scene; or 255 as the maximum value for a grayscale image) and rest of the pixels with non-movement information will remain zero.

Now, as per the above equation, if there is no moving scene in the next frame $I(x, y, 4)$ at pixel values (2,3) and (3,4)—then the new pixel values for (2,3) and (3,4) will be $H_\tau(x, y, t - 1) - 1$, i.e., the earlier value will be reduced or decayed by '1'. So, if we consider the maximum value as 255, then in this case, the new value will be $(255 - 1) = 254$. However, the new pixel value for (3,3) will remain the same. In this manner, we can find an image where the minimum pixel value will be '0', which means those pixel values having '0' have no moving information or it has been reduced to '0' since, there is no movement since long.

Now, instead of reducing the value by '1' for not having moving information in that specific pixel after having motion information before, we may find situations where it might be necessary to reduce more pixel values for each time—not having moving scene. Now, if δ defines the decay parameter of the MHI, we can write,

$$H_\tau(x, y, t) = \begin{cases} \tau & \text{if } \Psi = 1 \\ \max(0, H_\tau(x, y, t - 1) - \delta) & \text{otherwise} \end{cases} \quad (3.8)$$

Here, the value of the decay parameter (δ) can be 1 or more.

Note that the update function ($\Psi(x, y, t)$) is recursively called for every frame or set of consecutive frames that are considered or analyzed in that video scene. A final MHI image records the temporal history of motion in it. We can get the final MHI template as $H_\tau(x, y, t)$. It might be necessary to perform median filtering to smooth the MHIs and remove the salt-pepper noise; or, implementing a Gaussian filter for the same.

Meng et al. [318] show a comparative demonstration of the MHI and the *Modified Motion History Image* (modified-MHI) representations [305] in Fig. 3.3.

Fig. 3.3 A bird flying in the sky: the corresponding MHI representation (*mid-image*) and the Modified-MHI (*right-image*). It is evident that both representations can keep the information on motion flow or history. With kind permission from Springer Science+Business Media B.V.—from Meng et al. [318]

3.2.2.1 The MEI from the MHI

The MEI can also be generated from the MHI. Therefore, when we need to have the
MEI image, we just need to take the binarized version of the MEI of that moment.
The MEI is achieved by thresholding an MHI image above zero, as per the following
equation,

$$E_\tau(x, y, t) = \begin{cases} 1 & \text{if } H_\tau(x, y, t) \geq 1 \\ 0 & \text{otherwise} \end{cases} \tag{3.9}$$

It is noticeable that these representations are computed based on recursive manner,
where only latest information need to be stored and manipulated, and no history of
the previous images or their motion fields need to be stored nor manipulated, making
the computation both fast and space efficient [492].

3.2.2.2 Some Examples of MHI and MEI Images

Here, we present some images for the MHI and MEI for different actions. Figure 3.4
(top row) shows five MHI images up to different frame numbers for an action. The
corresponding Motion Energy Images up to that frame numbers are shown in Fig. 3.4
(bottom row) for the same action. The MHI/MEI images are shown for up to frame
10, 15, 34, 36, and 46. The action is taken from the Kaggle Gesture Challenge
'ChaLearn' Database [14].

Now, if we look at the images of Fig. 3.5 for the same action but with higher
value of δ (instead of 1, we use 10), we notice that a large amount of prior motion
information is missing as time elapses.

Lets consider another action to produce the MHI and MEI. In this case, the action
is a hand gesture. Figure 3.6 shows sequences of the MHI and MEI images according
to frame numbers (up to frame 10, 20, 26, 31, and 42).

Now, for action 2, the corresponding MHI values will be different if we consider
$\delta = 10$. Figure 3.7 shows these images.

Similarly, for another action, Fig. 3.8 shows another example. In this case, the
consecutive frame numbers are 20, 31, 40, 62, and 74. It is noticeable that if $\delta = 10$,
then the later MHI images can keep more motion information.

3.2.2.3 Other Dimensions on the MHI

Apart from the basic MHI/MEI paradigm—the developers of the MHI method have
analyzed it in different dimensions. For example, Davis [285] explains the gradient of
motion that can demonstrate the *direction* of movement based on the MHI. By now, it
is understandable that the MHI layers the successive silhouette differences in a such a
manner that motion from the silhouette boundary can be perceived in the gradient of
the MHI, which is very similar to the concept of normal flow. By convolving classic
gradient masks with the MHI, we can extract the directional motion information.

Fig. 3.4 Creation of MHI and MEI images for an action for different stages in terms of frame numbers

Fig. 3.5 Creation of MHI images for the above action with $\delta = 10$ instead of $\delta = 1$ for the above image. Note the impact of δ parameter

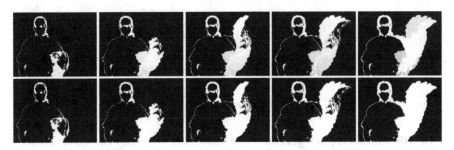

Fig. 3.6 Creation of MHI and MEI images for a hand gesture for different stages in terms of frame numbers 10, 20, 26, 31, and 42. These are taken when the value of δ is one

Fig. 3.7 Creation of MHI images for a hand gesture for different stages in terms of frame numbers 10, 20, 26, 31, and 42, while the value for δ is ten

Fig. 3.8 For the value $\delta = 10$, the impact of the training of recent past seems not enough

In his technical note, Davis [285] explains this where two resolutions—the original and a lower resolution—are considered for convolution. Multi-resolution allows the scope to handle more widespread gradients due to differing speeds of movement.

The following Sobel gradient masks are considered for the convolution,

$$F_x = \begin{bmatrix} -1 & 0 & 1 \\ -2 & 0 & 2 \\ -1 & 0 & 1 \end{bmatrix}$$

and

$$F_y = \begin{bmatrix} -1 & -1 & -1 \\ 0 & 0 & 0 \\ 1 & 2 & 1 \end{bmatrix}$$

Therefore, the gradient orientation for a pixel is,

$$\theta = arctan\frac{F_y}{F_x} \tag{3.10}$$

Bradski and Davis [369] generalize the basic MHI to directly encode actual time in a floating-point format, called *timed Motion History Image* (tMHI). In this presentation, new silhouette values are copied in with a floating-point timestamp in the format seconds.milliseconds. This MHI representation according to them,

$$tMHI_\delta(x, y) = \begin{cases} \tau & \text{if current silhouette at } (x, y) \\ 0 & \text{else if } tMHI_\delta(x, y) < (\tau - \delta) \end{cases} \tag{3.11}$$

where,
τ: Current timestamp.
δ: The maximum time duration constant (typically a few seconds) associated with the template.

It is claimed that this representation is independent of system speed or frame rate (within limits) so that a given gesture will cover the same MHI area at different capture rates [369]. A gradient of the tMHI is used to determine normal optical flow,

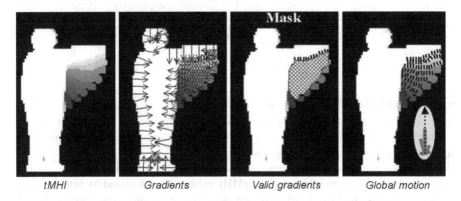

tMHI   Gradients   Valid gradients   Global motion

Fig. 3.9 tMHI image and gradient images of an upward arm movement, which are encoded in floating-point timestamps

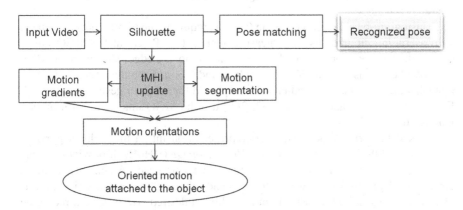

Fig. 3.10 A flowchart of the tMHI method

e.g., motion flow orthogonal to object boundaries. The motion is then segmented relative to object boundaries and the motion orientation of each region is obtained [369].

Figure 3.9 shows tMHI image of an upward arm movement encoded in floating-point timestamps yields a tMHI. The corresponding gradient, gradient mask, and global motion are also demonstrated in this image [369].

These are used for pose recognition, which is demonstrated by the flowchart shown in Fig. 3.10.

They also present a method of motion segmentation based on segmenting layered motion regions that are meaningfully connected to movements of the object of interest.

By weighting normalized tMHI, we can compute the global *Motion Gradient Orientation* (MGO). The MGO provides more influence to the most current motions within the template. The global weighted orientation can be computed by [369],

$$\theta_{gmo} = \theta_{ref} + \frac{\sum_{x,y} angDiff(\theta(x,y), \theta_{ref}) \times norm(\tau, \delta, t, MHI_\delta(x,y))}{\sum_{x,y} norm(\tau, \delta, MHI_\delta(x,y))}$$

(3.12)

where,

θ_{gmo}: The global motion orientation.

θ_{ref}: The base reference angle (peaked value in the histogram of orientations). A histogram-based reference angle (θ_{ref}) is required due to problems associated with averaging circular distance measurements.

$\theta(x, y)$: The motion orientation map found from gradient convolutions.

$norm(\tau, \delta, MHI_\delta(x, y))$: Normalized tMHI value. It is calculated by linearly normalizing the tMHI from 0 to 1 by employing the current timestamp (τ) and duration (δ).

$angDiff(\theta(x, y), \theta_{ref})$: Minimum, signed angular difference of an orientation from the reference angle.

A histogram-based reference angle (θ_{ref}) is required due to problems associated with averaging circular distance measurements [369]. Pixels in the MGO image encode the change in orientation between nearest moving edges shown on the MHI. The MGO contains information about *where* and *how* a motion has occurred [288]. Note that these orientation gradients are employed for action or gesture recognition. For example, Wong and Cipolla [287, 288] use the MGO images to form motion features for gesture recognition.

Davis [511] extend the basic MHI representation into a hierarchical pyramid format, called the *Hierarchical Motion History Image* (HHMI). It provides a mean of addressing the gradient calculation of multiple image speeds. An image pyramid is constructed by recursively low pass filtering and sub-sampling an image (i.e., power-of-2 reduction with anti-aliasing) until reaching a desired size of spatial reduction [511]. For this approach, for each pixel [511],

- Choose pyramid level that passes the gradient constraints.
- Compute motion from that level.
- Scale the result to the size of the original image.
- If multiple pyramid levels pass the gradient constraints, choose the level with the minimum acceptable temporal disparity (finest temporal resolution).

With a pyramid representation, two images having large motion displacements between them will have smaller displacements when compared at increasingly higher (reduced) pyramid levels [511]. The result is a hierarchy of motion fields where the resulting motion computed in each level is tuned to a particular speed and faster the speed—higher the level. Based on the orientations of the motion flow, a *Motion Orientation Histogram* (MOH) is also defined. Note that the Hierarchical Motion History Image is computationally inexpensive [294].

3.2.2.4 Approaches for the $D(x, y, t)$ or $\Psi(x, y, t)$

Detecting or segmenting or finding out the *moving-region of interest* from a video scene is very crucial for many vision-based approaches or applications; and it is the same for the Motion History Image method. Many vision-based moving object detection or extraction or segmentation or identification of its flow vectors can be done by employing one of the following approaches,

- (Static) background subtraction
- (Dynamic) background subtraction
- Frame subtraction or frame differencing
- Three-frame subtraction
- Optic flow or vector field
- Edge processing or accumulation
- Intensity-based segmentation
- Flesh color extraction
- Streakline and streak flow
- Dense particle trajectories or pathlines

Static background subtraction is the easiest approach among the above approaches. So, if the background is static and indoor environment with the presence of constant illumination—then the background subtraction can be done by subtracting the *background image* (where no *foreground* object of interest will be present) from each frame. This way, any moving object can be extracted as *foreground*. However, due to its simple approach which might be based on empirical *threshold* value, the background subtraction may not perform well in cluttered scene or cases where the object's color is relatively similar to the background color. A typical background subtraction approach can be,

$$I_{fg}(x, y, t) = I(x, y, t) - I_{bg}(x, y, t) \tag{3.13}$$

where,
$I_{bg}(x, y, t)$: Background image.
$I_{fg}(x, y, t)$: Foreground image or background subtracted image.

On the other hand, for a dynamic background, the subtraction method is difficult as each time, we need to *model* the *background* to do subtraction to get the moving object of interest. A smart background model should have the ability to capture very recent information about the image sequence, and to update this information continuously to capture fast changes in the scene background. If a background image is not fixed but changing due to, illumination changes (gradual changes vs. sudden changes, e.g., sudden presence of cloud in the sky); camera movement; presence of high-frequency background objects (e.g., tree branches, movement of leaves, sea waves, etc.); and changes in the background geometry (e.g., parked cars) [742]. At each new frame, each pixel can be classified as either foreground or background, and based on this approach we can determine foreground and background.

To build a background model, we can have one of the following background subtraction methods,

- Background as the average [72] or median [73] of the previous n frames. These approaches are fast though memory-wise taxing, as memory requirement is $n * size(frame)$.
- Background as running average, which can be defined as,

$$I_{bg_{i+1}}(x, y, t) = \alpha I(x, y, t) + (1 - \alpha) I_{bg_i}(x, y, t) \tag{3.14}$$

where, α: learning rate (a typical value is 0.05). It is difficult to get an optimum threshold value. There is no explicit approach to choose the threshold. Moreover, based on a predefined single value—these approaches fail to cope with multiple modal background distributions. Hence, we need to explore other approaches.
- Running Gaussian average [339]: This approach fits one Gaussian distribution (μ, σ) over the histogram that provides a background probability distribution function. This method also does not cope with multimodal background distributions.
- *Gaussian Mixture Model* (GMM) or *Mixture of k Gaussians* (MoG) [71, 340]: Considering mixture of k Gaussians $(\mu_i, \sigma_i, \omega_i)$, this model can cope with multimodal backgrounds, up to 3–5 pre-defined arbitrary modes. Here, all weights ω_i are updated and/or normalized at every new frame. However, concerns remain regarding initializing the Gaussians and updating these over period.
- *Kernel Density Estimators* (KDE) [344]: In this method, the background probability density function (PDF) is given by the histogram of the n most recent pixel values, each smoothed with a Gaussian kernel (sample-point density estimator). And if $PDF(X) > th$, where $X = (x, y)$ as a pixel value and th is the threshold value, the X pixel is classified as background. However, the memory requirement is high for KDE approach for background subtraction. Also, computing the kernel values is computationally taxing. By using Look-up Table (LUT), computational cost can be minimized.
- Mean-shift-based estimation [74]: It is a gradient-ascent method that is able to detect the modes of a multimodal distribution together with their covariance matrix. It is an iterative process where the step decreases toward convergence. Note that the iterative process may lead to very slow convergence and hence some sort of optimizations are necessary to make it faster. The memory requirement is $n * size(frame)$.
- *Sequential Kernel Density Approximation* (SKDA) [74]: This approach is based on combined estimation and propagation, where mean-shift mode detection from samples is used only at initialization stage; and later, modes are propagated by adapting them with new samples. Heuristic procedures are used for merging existing modes and the number of modes is not fixed beforehand. This approach is faster than *Kernel Density Estimators* (KDE)-based background subtraction method. It requires less memory.
- Eigen-backgrounds [75]: The Principal Compound Analysis (PCA) can be applied to a sequence of n frames to compute the eigen-backgrounds.

- Parametric model
- Non-parametric model

Given a new pixel sample, there are two alternative mechanisms to update a background [344],

- Selective update: Add the new sample to the model only if it is classified as a background sample.
- Blind update: Add the new sample to the model.

Some methods for background subtraction are available in [88–90, 335–344]. Frame differencing or frame to frame subtraction approaches are also used by many researchers, e.g., [542]. In the basic format, the frame differencing is also very simple to compute where consecutive frames are subtracted from each other and the moving regions are accumulated to get the foreground. However, similar to the background subtraction—the frame to frame subtraction methods may suffer from missing information. A proper selection of the threshold value is important for this case. Some approaches for frame differencing are [345–350]. A typical frame differencing approach can be,

$$I_{fg}(x, y, t) = I(x, y, t + 1) - I(x, y, t) \tag{3.15}$$

Various optical flow approaches are used for motion detection. Motion is represented as vectors originating or terminating at pixels in a digital image sequence. Some dominant approaches for determining optical flow are,

- Phase correlation (inverse of normalized cross-power spectrum)
- Block correlation (sum of absolute differences, normalized cross-correlation)
- Gradient constraint-based registration
- Lucas-Kanade (LK) method
- Horn-Schunck method

In another nomenclature, optical flow approaches can be categorized by,

- Region-based matching (e.g., correlation-based) approach
- Differential (gradient) approach
- Energy-based approach
- Phased-based approach

Region-based techniques compare patches of the image (or filtered image) at different disparities to determine the flow. Differential techniques compute velocity from spatio-temporal derivatives or a filtered version of the image. Differential optical flow, essentially, can be computed by the following basic procedure:

- Compute the *spatio-temporal intensity derivatives*. These derivatives are equivalent to measuring the velocities normal to the local intensity structures.
- Integrate normal velocities into full velocities. This integration can be done by,

– *Locally* by a least squares calculation [619]; or
– *Globally* via a regularization [353].

On the other hand, energy- and phase-based approaches apply velocity-tuned filters on the image sequence and extract the velocities from the filter's output. Some dominant optical flow methods are [351–359, 619]. For some applications, outlier can be reduced by employing *RANdom Sample Consensus* (RANSAC) [151], *Preemptive RANSAC* [84], and *PROgressive SAmple Consensus* (PROSAC) [83].

Optical flow methods by Horn and Schunck [353] and Lucas and Kanade [619] are two classical approaches, which are most widely used and studied. However, along with these two important methods, various other approaches are proposed to overcome some of the constraints and applicable in different applications. According to [354], optical flow methods can be split into the following divisions,

• The quadratic regularizer [353] is replaced by smoothness constraints allowing piecewise smooth results and discontinuities in the flow field [716–727].
• Optical flow methods based on joint motion estimation and motion segmentation [728–730].
• Optical flow methods motivated from robust statistics where outliers are penalized less severely [718, 731].
• Optical flow methods where problem of large displacements are tackled by coarse-to-fine strategies [457, 729, 731–733].
• Optical flow methods where problem of large displacements are tackled by non-linearized models [734, 735].
• Optical flow methods where by augmenting spatial approaches with an additional temporal dimension [718, 727, 728, 736–738].

3.2.2.5 Selection of τ

Problem statement: Actions at varying speeds.
The selection of a proper value for τ is critical for the construction of an MHI and the corresponding MEI images, especially for actions at varying speeds. According to [492], let's consider that the minimum and maximum duration that a movement may take are measured, denoted by τ_{min} and τ_{max}, respectively. If the actions are performed at varying speeds, we need to choose the most appropriate value for τ to compute the MHI and the MEI. A backward looking variable time window is employed initially by [492]. An algorithm is proposed to approximate for an appropriate value for τ over a wide range of τ. The basic steps of this algorithm as per [492] are,

• Compute a new MHI $H_\tau(x, y, t)$- at each time step by setting $\tau = \tau_{max}$. The τ_{max} is the longest-possible time window that we can consider for a dataset.
• Calculate $\Delta_\tau = (\tau_{max} - \tau_{min})/(n - 1)$. n is the number of temporal integration windows to be considered. Ideally, the value of n can be defined as, $n = \tau_{max} - \tau_{min} + 1$ resulting in a complete search of the time window between τ_{max} and τ_{min}. Computational limitations argue for a smaller n.

- A simple thresholding of the MHI values less than $\tau - \Delta_\tau$ generates $H_{\tau - \delta_\tau}(x, y, t)$ from $H_\tau(x, y, t)$:

$$
H_{\tau - \Delta_\tau}(x, y, t) = \begin{cases} (H_\tau(x, y, t) - \Delta_\tau) & \text{if } H_\tau(x, y, t) > \Delta_\tau \\ 0 & \text{otherwise} \end{cases} \tag{3.16}
$$

- Scale the $H_\tau(x, y, t)$ by $1/\tau$, which causes all the MHIs to range from 0 to 1 and provides invariance with respect to the speed of the movement.

3.2.3 Importance of the MHI and the MEI

We now understand the construction strategies of the MHI and the MEI representations. Now question may arise—do we really need the MHI and the MEI together for many and important applications. According to [492], both the MHI and the MEI is valuable even though the MEI can be constructed by thresholding the MHI. By showing some examples from some aerobics video dataset—and by creating the MHI and the MEI templates— they demonstrate that few actions have quite similar MEIs yet distinct MHIs. On the other hand, some actions have similar MHIs in terms of where the majority of image energy is located yet display quite distinct MEIs [492]. The MHI and the MEI projection functions capture two distinct characteristics of the motion—*how* and *where* respectively; and the shape descriptors of these two images discriminate differently.

In various applications, the MHI with the MEI, or only the MHI, or in some very few cases, only the MEI are employed for recognition, analysis, and other applications. However, for most of the recognition applications, both of the MHI and MEI are used due to the fact that both of these representations are important to distinguish various action classes. If we need only the presence of motion information or moving regions—then computing the Motion Energy Image might be good enough for some applications. On the other hand, the MHI is always useful not only to achieve the detected regions of a moving scene, but also to have the directions of the motion. However, we have to be careful on the basic limitations of these representations, for example, motion overwriting, multiple moving object in a scene, etc. because these constraints cannot be overcome easily.

However, in a variant of the MHI in 3D domain, Weinland et al. [279, 503, 531] demonstrate that both templates are not necessary. Although Davis and Bobick [492] clearly demonstrate and suggest in the original paper that the use of history and binary images together provide strong cues, the *Motion History Volume* (MHV) method—a view-invariant approach with the concept of the 2D MHI, experimentally show that there is no improvement in using a combination of *history*-template (MHV) and the binary *energy*-template (Motion Energy Volume, MEV) [531].

3.3 Limitations of the MHI Method

No method can single-handedly solve or address each and every problem related to action recognition. The Motion History Image representation or method is no exception! Therefore, the MHI and MEI representations have a number of constraints that limit its application in some cases. The key problems with the MHI method or the basic (MHI, MEI) representation [492] are,

- For a situation where one person partially occludes another, the MHI cannot perform. One solution for this problem is to employ multiple cameras. However, a multi-camera system may provide view-invariance property but with some added complexities.
- Another occlusion-related problem of the MHI representation is the 'motion self-occlusion' or 'motion overwriting'. For example, if someone is running from left to right direction (i.e., the created MHI will have brighter trace toward right direction) and then back from right to left direction (i.e., the created MHI will have brighter trace toward left direction)—we can notice vividly that the final MHI (and of course, the final MEI too) has no clue that the person ran from left to right direction earlier. So, this motion overwriting due to motion self-occlusion is problematic to the MHI method. In the context of motion analysis, this overwriting process leads to loss of important information and has to be eliminated [328]. Note that this typical occlusion differs from occlusions due to body part (e.g., hand), or another static object (e.g., tree), or moving object (e.g., another person, moving car), and this type of occlusion is mainly exclusive for the MHI method. Therefore, some solutions are tried to solve this problem by [317–320, 322, 327, 328, 530, 542], by considering multi-camera system or splitting optical flow vectors or considering multi-level history images.
- If more than one person appears in the view point, the MHI cannot distinguish them. This problem can be solved by using a tracking bounding box for each subject separately.
- If partial moving-body part is missing in the scene somehow, then those moving information will not be retained in the produced MHI template. This self-occlusion by human body part is difficult to solve. If we consider prior human model—then the simplicity of the MHI approach will be ruined, as model-based recognition approaches are sometimes computationally costly, as well as, difficult to recognize.
- Another problem arises when the motion of part of the body is not specified during a movement. For example, let's consider an action of *throwing a ball*. Whether the legs move is not determined by the movement itself, it may incorporate or induce huge variability in the statistical description of the temporal templates [492]. Therefore, if we want to extend the MHI method to such movements, we need to develop some mechanism to automatically either mask away regions of this type of motion or to always include them [492].
- Presence of camera motion disturbs the constructions of the original or expected moving scene. For example, if a person is jumping in a scene while the camera is moving—then the final MHI will cover more regions of movement, which is

wrong and unwanted. Hence, it is not easy to manage camera movement. However, a slight tilting or panning of a camera can be managed by post-processing of the available MHI image.

- As the MHI covers only the presence of movement, it cannot distinguish the actual action by a subject when the subject is performing the movement while locomotion. Some sort of tracking of the person (e.g., if the person walks while waving his hands and if *waving hands* is the action to be recognized) will be required. However, separating locomotion and action will be very difficult with the employment of the MHI only.

- According to the original paper on MHI by [492], a more sophisticated motion detection algorithm would increase robustness.

- In dynamic background, the MHI's performance is usually poor as the MHI incorporates anything that is moving [326]. Therefore, dynamic background subtraction technique or similar approach should be considered to have better segmentation of the target moving foreground extraction to construct an MHI.

- As developed, the method assumes all motion present in the image should be incorporated into the temporal templates [492]. Clearly, this approach would fail when two people are in the field of view [492]. To implement it in real-time system, they use a tracking bounding box that attempts to isolate the relevant motions.

- As the construction of the MHI is dependent on the τ—it cannot perform well with variable length of action sequences [559]. Note that a slow motion or action means longer video sequences, i.e., more number of frames for the same action compared to that of its faster motion. Therefore, an increase in the length τ of the temporal window is translated into a larger number of gray levels in the MHI. Encoding motion information in a gray-level image is thus limited by the maximum number of gray levels [328].

- The MHI provides a sort of directionality of an action and it presents the dominant motion direction only. However, from this information, we cannot be certain about the trajectory of that motion path [277]. Therefore, considering tracking algorithm would be beneficial if tracking is necessary for some applications.

- When one person partially occludes another, making separation difficult, if not impossible by the MHI [492]. By using multiple cameras, improved results are expected. As occlusion is view angle specific, multiple cameras may reduce the chance of occlusion. However, for some actions, employment of multi-cameras system may provide false recognition. For monitoring situations, an overhead camera can be employed to select which ground-based cameras have a clear view of a subject and to specify (assuming loose calibration) where the subject would appear in each image [492].

- If we consider the MHI method that incorporates recognizing action classes by considering the MHI and MEI representations, then due to its template-based recognition approach, we notice limitation of the MHI method. It is constrained by token- or label-based recognition [323, 511].

- Due to the overwriting phenomenon presented above, the MHI template is not applicable for the analysis of periodic human motion [328].

- Irregularities in human actions typically occur either in speed or orientation [328]. The MHI image cannot incorporate or manage these irregularities in motion [328].
- Though the MHI is employed for various gesture recognition as well as action/gait recognition, it cannot perform well for gestures or actions, which have more resemblances. It cannot significantly distinguish among similar actions [360]. There are some very similar gestures or signals, especially in sign language. On the other hand, some actions produce almost similar MHI or MEI representations from which we cannot recognize those actions easily, e.g., walking, jogging, and running.

3.4 MHI and its Variants: 2D/3D

This section presents the approaches and methods that have exploited the Motion History Image method or the MHI/MEI representations in its original format, or modified version of these. In the section where the applications of the MHI are presented, we present some of these methods only with applications. Here, we engage our efforts to point out the ways the MHI is employed and modified to develop a new method. These concepts will be helpful for readers to ponder on how to improve from a method or representation to a new method or presentation, and how these can be applicable to new applications in smarter manners.

3.4.1 View-Based MHI and its Variants

The *Mean Shift Embedded Particle Filter* (MSEPF) is employed for tracking the trajectories of hand gestures by Shan et al. [326]. They consider the MHI representation only for motion extraction in different manners. The MSEPF has the following steps—propagation, weighting, mean shift searching, selective resampling for 20 particles only, whereas the conventional particle filter requires about 150 particles for the same experiments. The MHI for hand gesture is created based on the hand tracking results. Spatial trajectories are retained in a static image, and the trajectories are called *Temporal Template-Based Trajectories* (TTBT) [326]. The TTBT extent temporal templates by introducing trajectories, and avoid the problems of temporal templates. It contains explicit spatio-temporal information of hand motion and since the TTBT are created from hand tracking results, the process does not demand static background and work well in real world situations [326]. This representation is different than the MHI. There are many random motion regions in background, which will influence template matching for recognition for the case of the MHI, especially in applications of hand gesture recognition, because for the MHI, the global description loses motion characteristics [326]. For feature vector, seven Hu invariants [496] are used to describe the shape of the TTBT. A two-layer classifier is used where in the first layer, the classification is done based on the Hu invariants and then in

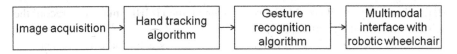

Fig. 3.11 A flowchart of the Temporal Template-Based Trajectories (TTBT)-based method

the second stage, it is accomplished based on displacement angles and orientation angles.

Figure 3.11 shows flowchart of this process.

Meng et al. [293] develop a simple system based on the SVM classifier and the MHI representations, which is implemented on a reconfigurable embedded computer vision architecture for real-time gesture recognition. The proposed method is called the *Hierarchical Motion History Histogram* (HMHH) [293, 317–320]. This representation retains more motion information than the MHI, and also remains computationally less-expensive [293]. Now, we briefly present the HMHH method. Let's consider the grayscale values of any pixel (say, pixel at (10,20)) of an MHI image for consecutive frames of a video sequence. Now, if some action happened at frame k on pixel (x, y), then $D(x, y, k) = 1$, otherwise $D(x, y, k) = 0$. Let's assume that the locations of these pixels are $(10, 20), (10, 21), (10, 22), \ldots, (10, 40)$. For a pixel (x, y), the motion mask $D(x, y, :)$ of this pixel is a binary sequence of,

$$D(x, y, :) = (b_1, b_2, \ldots, b_N); b_i \in 0, 1 \tag{3.17}$$

where, $N + 1$ is the total number of frames. Therefore, for a pixel $(10, 20)$, the motion mask $D(10, 20, :)$ constitutes a sequence of 0s and 1s. However, the MHI can only retain the latest 1 in the sequence and hence, earlier motion information are overwritten by any later information, which causes missing of motion information. On the contrary, the HMHH representation is developed to overcome this constraint and retain all moving information in stages. The HMHH defines some patterns P_i in the motion mask $(D(x, y, :))$ of sequence, based on the number of connected 1 in the sequence. For example,

$$P_i = 010, P_2 = 0110, P_3 = 01110, \ldots, P_M = 01 \ldots 10 \text{ total number of 1 is } M \tag{3.18}$$

Now, they define a subsequence $C_i = b_{n1}, b_{n2}, \ldots, b_{ni}$, and denote the set of all sub-sequences of $D(x, y, :)$ as $\Omega D(x, y, :)$. For every pixel, they count the number of occurrences of each specific pattern P_i in the sequence of $D(x, y, :)$. It can be defined by,

$$HMHH(x, y, P_i) = \sum_j \mathbf{1}_{C_j = P_i | C_j \in \Omega D(x, y, :)} \tag{3.19}$$

where, $\mathbf{1}$ is called as an indicator function. From each pattern P_i, they construct a grayscale image, called Motion History Histogram (MHH). If we consider four patterns, then we can have four MHH images. Finally, all MHH images construct a Hierarchical Motion History Histogram (HMHH) image. Unlike the hierarchical

MHI, where only small size MHIs were obtained, the HMHH image can record the rich information of an action [317].

However, the size of the HMHH representation is a bit large to present to a classifier and hence a more compact representation is developed where (similar to the MEI from the MHI) a binarized version of each MHH is computed first,

$$MHH_b(x, y, P_i) = \begin{cases} 1 & \text{if } MHH(x, y, P_i) > 0 \\ 0 & \text{otherwise} \end{cases} \tag{3.20}$$

According to [317], take sum of each row of $MHH_b(x, y, P_i)$ to give a vector of size X rows; and sum of each column to have another vector of size Y rows. Thus by using all M levels in the binarized $MHH(x, y, P_i)$ hierarchy, a vector $(M*(X+Y))$ is produced called *Motion Geometric Distribution* (MGD),

$$MGD = \sum_x MHH_b(x, y, P_i), \sum_y MHH_b(x, y, P_i) \tag{3.21}$$

where, i = 1, 2, ..., M. The Support Vector Machine (SVM) is used for classification.

Figure 3.12 [293] shows five patterns of the HMHH for six actions for the KTH dataset. We can notice that as the number of patterns increases, the motion information ceases. Therefore, it depends on actions or applications to determine the number of patterns to exploit.

Meng et al. [293] combine various features along with their *Motion History Histogram* (MHH) images for recognition. Compact feature vector is extracted from input video image–based on the MHI, the Modified Motion History Image [305], the *Motion Gradient Orientation* (MGO), and the MHH. Figure 3.13 shows a flow diagram of this approach [293].

These feature vectors are compressed by dimension reduction methods. They employ histogram of the MHI; sub-sampling (or down-sampling) on the MHI, the modified-MHI, the MGO and the MHH; and *Motion Geometric Distribution* (MGD). Finally, Support Vector Machine (SVM) is used as classifier to recognize actions from the KTH dataset. Based on their experiments with different combinations of these features, the following results are achieved as shown in Table 3.1 for the KTH dataset.

The MHI is employed for gesture recognition for interaction with handicapped people [294]. In this approach the MHI for each gesture, motion orientation histogram vector is extracted for hand gesture recognition.

Action characteristics by MHIs for some hand gesture recognition and four different actions (i.e., jumping, squatting, limping, and walking) are modeled by [292]. They introduce *discriminative actions*, which describe the usefulness of the fundamental units in distinguishing between events. The action characteristics are modeled using Motion History Images. *Fisher Discriminant Analysis* (FDA) is used.

Reference [329] propose a simple approach to detect a suspicious person in a parking-lot by computing the trajectories based on the MHI images. Abnormalities are defined based on various profiles of changes in velocity and in acceleration from

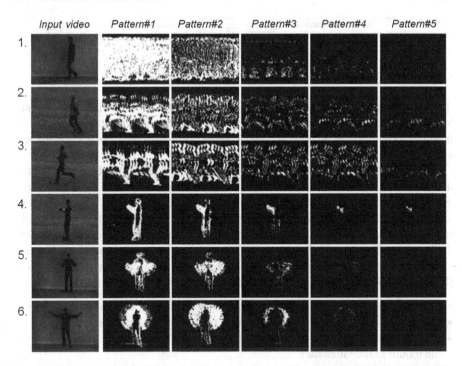

Fig. 3.12 HMHH representations for five patterns. Six actions are taken from the KTH dataset. With kind permission from Springer Science+Business Media B.V.—from Meng et al. [293], Chap. 7

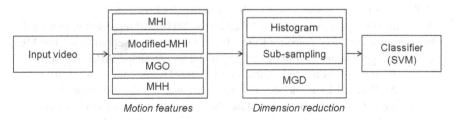

Fig. 3.13 A simple flow diagram of the compact approach of multiple features by [293]

Table 3.1 Average recognition results for KTH dataset, considering some MHI-based motion features	Motion features	Average recognition rate (in %)
	MHI	63.50
	MHI (sub-sampled)	62.95
	Histogram of MHI	54.80
	MHH (sub-sampled)	69.55
	MGD	72.10
	MGD + Histogram of MHI	80.30

Fig. 3.14 A flow diagram of visual speech recognition by the MHI

the MHI. The profiles are in the category of highest MHI, average MHI, and median MHI values for each subject. A *Modified Probabilistic Neural Network* (MPNN) is introduced that can achieve reliable classification of some visual surveillance applications.

References [532, 533] apply the MHI in visual speech recognition where they decompose MHI images into wavelet sub-images using *Stationary Wavelet Transform* (SWT). Normalization of the intensity values of the MHI is done between 0 and 1 to minimize the difference in MHIs produced from video data of different rapidity of speech. The MHI demonstrates its ability to remove static elements from the sequence of images and preserves the short duration complex mouth movement [532]. The MHI is a view-sensitive motion representation technique. Hence, as per [533] the MHI generated from the sequence of images is dependent on,

- Position of the speaker's mouth normal to the camera optical axis.
- Orientation of the speaker's face with respect to the video camera.
- Distance of the speaker's mouth from the camera that changes the scale or size of the mouth in the video data.
- Small variation of the mouth movement of the speaker while uttering the same consonant. The Stationary Wavelet Transform is used to denoise and to minimize the variations between the different MHIs of the same consonant.

A flow diagram of the approach is shown in Fig. 3.14.

Vili et al. [327] propose a method based on the MHI/MEI representation with the only difference that they consider to use the silhouette representation for the MEI calculation to get a better overall description of the human shape. After that the *Local Binary Pattern* (LBP) is used to characterize both MHI and MEI. Therefore, inherently, the MHI-based LBP encodes the information about the direction of motion; whereas, the MEI-based LBP codes describe the combination of overall pose and shape of motion. As changes in the gray levels of the MHI encode the motion, the outer edges of the MHI may be misleading as texture is considered [327]. In these areas there is no useful motion information and so the non-moving pixels having zero value should not be included in the calculation of the LBP. That's why, they limit the calculation of the LBP features to the non-monotonous area within the MHI template.

One of the constraints of the LBP is that it can only contain information about the local spatial structure—not the overall structure of a motion. Hence, instead of keeping and considering the MHI as its entirety, the MHI is split into four sub-regions through the centroid of the silhouette. Now, each sub-region may not have enough motion cues in it and hence, a weighting scheme is proposed based on the ratio of the area of non-zero pixels that the MHI subimage (R_i where $i = 4$) contains to the area of non-zero pixels in the whole image. It is defined as,

Fig. 3.15 A typical system flow diagram of [324]

$$w_i = \frac{area(R_i)}{\sum_j area(R_j)} \tag{3.22}$$

The calculation of LBP features from the MEI is performed only on these non-monotonous areas with equal weights for each subimage. Finally, these temporal aspects are modeled with the *Hidden Markov Models* (HMMs).

A silhouette-based action modeling for recognition by [324] is modeled by employing the MHI directly as the input feature of the actions. These images are projected into a new subspace by means of the Kohonen *Self Organizing feature Map* (SOM). A specific SOM is trained for every action, grouping viewpoint (spatial), and movement (temporal) in a principal manifold. Actions are recognized by a Maximum Likelihood (ML) classifier over all specific-action SOMs.

A typical flow diagram of this approach is shown in Fig. 3.15.

Reference [308] propose an adaptive camera navigation model for video surveillance. This model can automatically learn locations of *activity regions of interest*. It measures activity from the MHI at each view across the full viewable field of a PTZ camera. From the MHI images, it searches for potential candidates for any human activity. All MHI blobs that are selected as candidate human activity are passed to a classification stage for stricter evaluation of translating motion [308].

Classification of a candidate MHI blob (i.e., translating vs. noise) is done by using a histogram similarity measure to quantify the degree of match between the normalized candidate MHI blob timestamp distribution and the ideal/expected timestamp distribution (uniform) for that blob, where normalization is based on blob size. Then MHI reduction is done by removing noise pixels by considering the gradient magnitude image of the MHI blob. Next, a global *activity map* is created for a camera's full viewable field using the local activity measures. Finally, navigation is done for four cases by using three Pelco Spectra III SE series dome cameras that are mounted outdoors on three different university campus buildings, two of which have overlapping views. The cameras are mounted at different heights. The experimental results are promising.

Basic steps for this approach is shown in Fig. 3.16 [308].

Reference [374] propose a Bayesian framework for action recognition based on *psycho-kinesiological* observations, namely, the ballistic nature of human movements. The Bayesian framework leads to an efficient algorithm for temporally segmenting videos into ballistic movements. They show that the consideration of ballistic dynamics enhances the performance of the Motion History Image feature [374].

Gait recognition is one of the recent biometrics by which individuals can be recognized by the way they walk. There are different methods and representations for gait recognition. Some of the key forms are developed at the top of the MHI and the

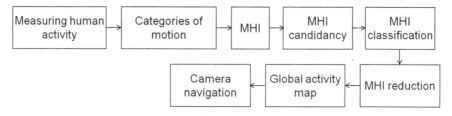

Fig. 3.16 Basic steps for video surveillance method by [308]

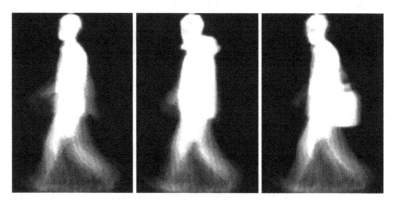

Fig. 3.17 The GEI images of a person under different carrying and clothing conditions; in this case—sequentially—*normal gait, carrying a bag*, and *wearing a coat*. With kind permission from Springer Science+Business Media B.V.—from Bashir et al. [300], Fig. 1, Springer, 2008

MEI representations. The Gait Energy Image (GEI) [297, 298] is developed for gait analysis. Silhouettes are extracted from original human walking sequences for this purpose. Size normalization (proportionally resizing each silhouette image so that all silhouettes have the same height) and horizontal alignment (centering the upper half silhouette part with respect to its horizontal centroid) are done as silhouette preprocessing steps. Then based on these preprocessed binary gait silhouette images $B_t(x, y)$ at time t in a video sequence, the gray-level Gait Energy Image $GEI(x, y)$ is developed,

$$GEI(x, y) = \frac{1}{N} \sum_{t=1}^{N} B_t(x, y) \tag{3.23}$$

where,
N is the number of frames in the complete cycle(s) of a silhouette sequence,
t is the frame number in the sequence (moment of time), and x and y are values in the 2D image coordinate [298].
Figure 3.17 shows some gait images as the GEI images.

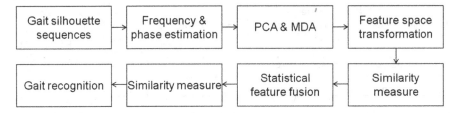

Fig. 3.18 A block diagram of the GEI method for gait recognition

Some basic properties of the GEI are [298],

- The GEI reflects major shapes of silhouettes and their changes over the gait cycle.
- The GEI is preferred as each silhouette image is the space-normalized energy image of human walking at this moment.
- The GEI is the *time-normalized accumulative energy image* of human walking in the complete cycle(s).
- A pixel with higher intensity value in GEI means that human walking occurs more frequently at this position (i.e., with higher energy).
- As compared to the MHI/MHI, the GEI targets specific normal human walking representation.
- The GEI representation saves both storage space and computation time for recognition.
- It is less sensitive to silhouette noise in individual frames.

The GEI has *static areas* which are little-moving body parts that move little during a walking cycle (e.g., head, torso), and has highest intensity values (white). These regions represent body shape and stance. On the other hand, the pixels with intensity values between the highest and lowest number (gray) correspond to body parts that move constantly (e.g., lower parts of legs and arms) [299]. This later regions are the most important part, called *dynamic areas* of a GEI. The dynamic areas are invariant to the appearance of an individual; they seem to be the most informative part of the GEI representation for human identification [299]. When a series of training GEI templates (real or synthetic) for each individual are obtained, dimensionality reduction methods are used to reduce dimensions. The Principal Component Analysis (PCA) and Multiple Discriminant Analysis (MDA) are employed. A statistical feature fusion is proposed. The block diagram shows the process of recognition of gaits based on the GEI images (Fig. 3.18).

The GEI is also exploited by [43–45, 299–301, 361] for gait recognition. The Gait Energy Image (GEI) is used by [361] along with the *Co-evolutionary Genetic Programming* (CGP) to recognize some actions. Hu invariants and normalized histogram bins are extracted from the original GEIs as input features. The Co-evolutionary Genetic Programming reduces the dimensionality of the features and learns the classifiers. *Majority voting* is applied to the CGP to improve the overall performance. Reference [301] consider the Gabor phase spectrum of the GEI as input feature. It is embedded into a low dimensional manifold by locality preserving projections to perform classification.

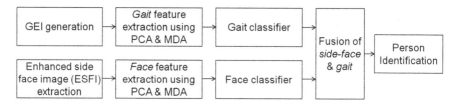

Fig. 3.19 A flow diagram of an integrated gait- and face-based recognition method at a distance

Liu et al. [44] also exploit the GEI. They assess the quality of silhouette sequences to determine the contribution of each GEI for classification according to the quality of GEI. Reference [43] apply the wavelet decomposition of GEI to infrared thermal gait recognition. The infrared gait sequences are robust to the covariates of holding a ball and loading packages. Multi-variables gait feature is extracted according to a novel method combining integral model and simplified model. Also the wavelet transform, invariant moments and skeleton theory are used to extract gait features [43]. They use Support Vector machine (SVM) for classifying gaits from thermal imagery with promising results.

Zhou and Bhanu incorporate the GEI along with *Enhanced Side-Face Images* (ESFI) to integrate gait and face for human recognition at a distance [45]. The basic recognition approach is similar to the above but with the incorporation of the side-face analysis and recognition. A simple flow diagram of this approach is shown in Fig. 3.19.

Feature learning is based on the combination of PCA and MDA for both side-face features and GEI-based features. PCA reduces the dimension of the feature space, and MDA automatically identifies the most discriminating features [45].

Another method for gait recognition is developed by Liu and Zheng [330] called the Gait History Image (GHI), similar to the concept of the MHI representation. The $GHI(x, y)$ inherits the idea of the MHI, where the temporal information and the spatial information can be recorded in both cases. The $GHI(x, y)$ preserves the temporal information besides the spatial information. It can overcome the shortcoming of no temporal variation in the $GEI(x, y)$ [42, 302]. The $GHI(x, y)$ can be defined as,

$$GHI(x, y) = \begin{cases} \tau & \text{if } S(x, y) = 1 \\ \sum_{t=1}^{\tau} D(x, y, t)(t - 1) & \text{otherwise} \end{cases} \quad (3.24)$$

where,

$$S(x, y) = \begin{cases} 1 & \text{if } GEI(x, y) \geq th \\ 0 & \text{otherwise} \end{cases} \quad (3.25)$$

where, the threshold $th = max(GHI(x, y)) * 80$. It can be noted that the GHI representation can model gaits in a more comprehensive manner than similar other temporal template methods. The GHI can represent the static and dynamic characteristics, as well as the spatial and temporal variations of various gaits.

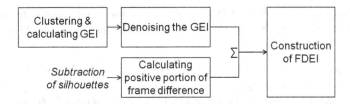

Fig. 3.20 A system flow diagram of the construction of the Frame Difference Energy Image (FDEI)

The Frame Difference *Energy* Image (FDEI) is proposed by [42] based on the GEI and the GHI to address the problem of silhouette incompleteness. They calculate the positive portion of frame difference as positive values of the subtraction between the current frame and the previous frame. The FDEI is defined as the summation of the GEI and the positive portion [42]. The FDEI representation can preserve the kinetic and static information of each frame, even when the silhouettes are incomplete. A system flow diagram of the construction of the FDEI is shown in Fig. 3.20.

Here, the silhouettes of the gait sequences are clustered and the Gait Energy Image (GEI) is computed. Next, the GEI of the cth cluster $GEI_c(x, y)$ is denoised to determine the *Dominant Energy Image* (DEI), according to the following equation,

$$DEI_c(x, y) = \begin{cases} GEI_c(x, y) & \text{if } GEI_c(x, y) \geq T \\ 0 & \text{otherwise} \end{cases} \tag{3.26}$$

The threshold T varies with different cycles or subjects, depending on the quality of the silhouettes. In the next step, *Positive Portion of Frame Difference* is obtained by setting the negative pixel values of the frame difference to zero, according to,

$$PPFD(x, y, t) = \begin{cases} 0 & \text{if } D(x, y, t) \geq D(x, y, t-1) \\ D(x, y, t) - D(x, y, t-1) & \text{otherwise} \end{cases}$$
$$\tag{3.27}$$

where,

$D(x, y, t)$ is silhouettes.

When $t = 1$, the $D(x, y, t-1)$ is set to the last frame of the cycle.

If $D(x, y, t)$ is incomplete and $D(x, y, t-1)$ is complete, then $PPFD(x, y, t)$ will contain the missing and movement portions, else, it only embodies the movement portions [42]. Finally, we construct the $FDEI(x, y, t)$ as the summation of the positive portion of the frame difference $PPFD(x, y, t)$ and the corresponding cluster's DEI $DEI_c(x, y, t)$. Experimental results are based on the CMU Mobo gait database with synthesized occlusions and the CASIA gait database (dataset B).

Gait features are extracted for gait recognition using the Frame Difference *History* Image (FDHI) [41]. After accomplishing sequence-based silhouette normalization and an alignment pre-processing step, the FDHI features are constructed. Two types of FDHI templates are extracted. Principal Component Analysis (PCA) followed by

Linear Discriminant Analysis (LDA) are employed for dimensional reduction. The k-Nearest Neighbor (KNN) classifiers and a fusion technique are used for classification.

Chandrashekhar and Venkatesh [315] propose the *Action Energy Image* (AEI) for human activity recognition. They consider pixel intensity at each pixel in XY direction of the spatio-temporal volume as a $1D$ function of time $f_{xy}(n)$ and perform $1D$ Fourier analysis of this signal at each xy,

$$F_{xy}(k) = \sum_{n=1}^{N} f_{xy}(n) * e^{-\frac{j*2\pi*k*n}{N}} \tag{3.28}$$

The AEIs are computed by averaging silhouettes. The MEI captures only *where* the motion occurred, but the AEI captures *where* and *how* much the motion occurred. PCA is employed on the AEIs. The AEI incorporates the information about both structure and motion.

The *Gait Moment Image* (GMI) is proposed by [303], which is the gait probability image at each key moment of all gait cycles. The corresponding gait images at a key moment are averaged as the GEI of this key moment. However, it is not easy for GMI to select key moments from cycles with different periods [42]. For a subject h, the GMI representation can be defined at the kth key moment as,

$$GMI_h(x, y, k) = \frac{1}{C_h} \sum_{c=1}^{C_h} S(x, y, k) \tag{3.29}$$

where,
C_h: Number of gait cycles in the current walking sequence of the subject h;
$S(x, y, k)$: Original silhouette image at the kth key moment in the cth gait cycle.

Now, we calculate the difference image between the original silhouette images and the gait moment images,

$$om(x, y, k) = \frac{1}{C_h} \sum_{c=1}^{C_h} |S(x, y, k) - GMI(x, y, k)| \tag{3.30}$$

The *Moment Deviation Image* (MDI) is also developed by using silhouette images and the GMIs. As a good complement of the $GEI(x, y)$, the MDI provides more motion features than the $GEI(x, y)$. In order to define an MDI image, we need to know the *gait period* p_h of a subject. The final Moment Deviation Image (MDI) can be calculated from the following equation in a recursive manner,

$$MDI(x, y, k) = \begin{cases} max(MDI(x, y, k - 1) - 255/p, 0) & \text{if } om(x, y, k) = 0 \\ max(MDI(x, y, k - 1), om(x, y, k)) & \text{otherwise} \end{cases} \tag{3.31}$$

It represents a kind of accumulation of the deviations of original silhouette images from moment probability images [303]. Both MDI and $GEI(x, y)$ are utilized to present a subject.

Two other representations, named *Average Motion Energy* (AME) and *Mean Motion Shape* (MMS) are proposed by [612] for activity recognition. The MMS is proposed based on shapes, not silhouettes. Supervised pattern classification techniques using various distance measures are used for recognition [612]. The AME can be computed from a set of aligned silhouettes $S(x, y, t)$,

$$AME(x, y) = \frac{1}{T} \sum_{t=1}^{T} S(x, y, t) \tag{3.32}$$

where, T: Number of frames. The pixel value in $AME(x, y)$ represents the intensity at position (x, y). References [309, 314, 362] present a representation from silhouettes called *Silhouette Energy Image* (SEI), which is exactly the same as the AME image.

The process of generating the AME is computationally inexpensive and can be employed in real-time applications [304]. However, the AME has to face the computation efficiency problem with the increasing number of database templates. This AME is computed exactly the similar manner of the computation of the GEI and according to [304], the AME and the GEI are same representations. The AME is exploited for action recognition, whereas the GEI method is used for gait recognition.

Yu et al. [304] propose a histogram-based approach that can efficiently compute the similarity among patterns. The Average Motion Energy image is obtained based on the extracted motion period and converted into a new representation called *Motion Energy Histogram* (MEH). In fact, the AME can be considered as a two-dimensional histogram whose bin value represents the frequency on position (x, y) during time interval t. Hence, the MEH can be defined based on the AME as,

$$MEH = \frac{AME(x, y)}{\sum_{x, y \in AME} AME(x, y)} \tag{3.33}$$

Then quadtree decomposition is performed on the MEH to construct the *Multiresolution Motion Energy Histogram* (MRMEH). The MRMEH is constructed by summing certain bins at higher resolution level. Periodic actions and gaits are recognized by this approach. Figure 3.21 shows a system diagram of this method.

Jin et al. [306] propose an *Intra Motion History Image* (IMHI) based on the MHI representation for generating inside moving parts of moving scene. In this approach, *Rear Motion History Image* (RMHI) and *Front Motion History Image* (FMHI) are considered that represent how motion is evolved—similar to the concept of the MHI. Afterwards, motion vectors with orientation and magnitude are generated from the chamfer distance; and the IMHI is produced [306].

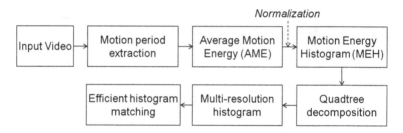

Fig. 3.21 A flowchart of the Multi-resolution Motion Energy Histogram (MRMEH) method

References [309, 314, 362] present the *Silhouette Energy Image* (SEI) as mentioned with the AME; and the *Silhouette History Image* (SHI). The SHI image refers to the shape variation of the image sequence in time [309]. It depicts how the silhouette of an image sequence is moving, and represents the global motion orientation of an action at any instant of time. Compare to the MHI, the SHI can demonstrate the body shape of the person at present state, as well as the person's global motion orientation or change. In this case, the brighter region represents the recency of the global human body shape [309].

Edges are considered for an enhanced version of the MHI representation by [311, 316]. They propose an *Edge Motion History Image* (EMHI) for special applications, e.g., video shots classification in news and sports videos with complex background scenes. For these cases, the background is not easy to be extracted and hence, the conventional MHI template is not easy to be produced. Moreover, stereo depth information is usually not available in video data either [316]. Therefore, the proposed EMHI representation exploits edge information detected in each frame image instead of silhouettes or background subtracted images. The EMHI can be computed according to,

$$EMHI_\tau(x, y, t) = \begin{cases} \tau & \text{if } E_t(x, y) = 1 \\ \max(0, EMHI_\tau(x, y, t - 1) - 1) & \text{otherwise} \end{cases} \quad (3.34)$$

where, $E_t(x, y)$: A binary value that indicate whether a pixel (x, y) is located on an edge at time t. The EMHI compresses the temporal dimensions using binomial model of bounded edge frequency at each pixel to obtain a low dimensional feature vector [316]. The computation of the EMHI is faster than any optical flow-based approach. Another edge-based MHI approach is proposed by [61], where they accumulate edges to produce *Edge-Accumulated History Image* (EHI). Note that edge-based MHI approaches suffer from constraints related to scale sensitivity and noises in edge detection [311]. In another approach, instead of edges, contours in multiple frames represent a spatial-temporal volume by Yilmaz and Shah [608].

The *Multiple-level Motion History Image* (MMHI) method is proposed by [322, 530] where they record motion history at multiple time intervals, hence the name *multi-level MHIs*. It creates all MHIs to have a fixed number of history levels n. So, each image sequence is sampled to $(n + 1)$ frames. We can compute the MMHI

$(MMHI_t(x, y, t))$ by,

$$MMHI_t(x, y, t) = \begin{cases} s * t & \text{if } \Psi(x, y, t) = 1 \\ MMHI_t(x, y, t - 1) & \text{otherwise} \end{cases} \quad (3.35)$$

where,
$s = (255/n)$: Intensity step between two history levels; and $MMHI_t(x, y, t) = 0$
for $t \leq 0$. This equation is computed iteratively for $t = 1, \ldots, n + 1$. The MMHI
representation is employed for the detection of facial action units (AU) [530] and
later for action recognition. However, the recognition results are found to be poor.
The MMHI uses a simple bit-wise coding scheme. For example, if a motion occurs
at time t at pixel location (x, y), it adds 2^{t-1} to the old motion value of the MMHI
as follows,

$$MMHI(x, y, t) = MMHI(x, y, t - 1) + \Psi(x, y, t).2^{t-1}. \quad (3.36)$$

Due to the bitwise coding scheme, it is possible to separate multiple actions
occurring at the same position [530]. Finally, from these templates, classification is
done by classifier schemes: a two-stage classifier combining a k-Nearest Neighbor
and a rule-based classifier; and a *Sparse Network of Winnows* (SNoW) classifier.
Using MMI-Face database and Cohn-Kanade database, the basic MHI representation
outperforms the proposed MMHI representation. The employed distance measure
makes it difficult to find the desired nearest neighbor of a sample when multiple levels
are activated on the same position in a MMHI [530]. However, it is claimed that the
MMHI data representation can offer many benefits in applications where confusions
caused by motion self-occlusion are common (e.g., in hand gesture recognition,
waving the hand is often confused with moving the hand from left to right only) by
[530].

One of the concerns of the MHI representation is that—at each pixel location,
explicit information about its past is lost when current changes are updated to the
model with their corresponding MHI values *jumping* to the maximal value [331].
Hence, Ng and Gong [289] propose the *Pixel Signal Energy* (PSE) in order to mitigate
this problem. It can measure the mean magnitude of pixel-level temporal energy over
a period of time by employing a backward window, whose size is determined by the
number of stored frames [290]. The pixel energy P_e is measured from the response
of pairs of quadrature filters as,

$$P_e(x, y, t) = \left[\sum_{i=0}^{2v} g(\tfrac{ct \times (i-v)}{v})(x, y, t - i) \right]^2 + \left[\sum_{i=0}^{2v} h(\tfrac{ct \times (i-v)}{v})(x, y, t - i) \right]^2 \quad (3.37)$$

where,
v: Temporal width of quadrature filters.
ct: Cut-off filter of a value of 3.5.
Filter masks are—
$g(y) = \eta(2y^2 - 1)e^{-y^2}$

Fig. 3.22 A flowchart of the Motion Flow History (MFH) method

$$h(y) = \kappa y + \lambda y^3 e^{-y^2}$$
$$\eta = 0.9213$$
$$\kappa = -2.205$$
$$\lambda = 0.978$$

Pixel energy extracts the signature of change occurring at any time instant [289]. Pixel signal energy, computed from the local color history of the pixel, provides a condensed temporal measure of change. In a similar pattern, *Pixel Change History* (PCH) [331] is proposed that measures the multi-scale temporal changes at each pixel. A PCH image becomes an MHI image if its accumulation factor is set to 1. Similar to that of the PSE [289], a PCH can also capture a zero-order pixel-level change, i.e., the mean magnitude of change over time [331].

Another motion representation method called the *Motion Flow History* (MFH) [321, 323] is proposed from compressed video to characterize actions. The difference between the MHI and the MFH is that the former representation provides temporal information of a motion, whereas, the MFH can quantify the motion at the image plane. The MFH gives the information about the extent of the motion at each macroblock, i.e., *where* and *how much* the motion occurred. We can construct the MFH from non-zero P-frame motion vectors, as per the following equation,

$$MFH_d(k,l) = \begin{cases} m_d^{kl}(\tau) & \text{if } E(m_d^{kl}(\tau)) < T_r \\ M(m_d^{kl}(\tau)) & \text{otherwise} \end{cases} \tag{3.38}$$

where, $E(m_d^{kl}(\tau)) = \|m_d^{kl}(\tau) - med(m_d^{kl}(\tau) \cdots m_d^{kl}(\tau - \alpha))\|^2$.
$M(m_d^{kl}(\tau)) = med(m_d^{kl}(\tau) \cdots m_d^{kl}(\tau\alpha))$.
$med()$: Median filter.
$m_d^{kl}(\tau)$ can be horizontal (m_x) component or vertical (m_y) component of motion vector located at kth row and lth column in frame τ.
α: It is the number of previous P-frames to be considered for median filtering (a typical range for α is 3-5) [323].
$E()$: This function checks the reliability of the current motion vector with respect to previous non-zero motion vectors.
T_r: Threshold value which ensures that no reliable motion vector of the MFH will be replaced by a recent noisy motion vector.

From the computed MFH template, three different features are extracted, namely— affine feature, projected 1D feature and 2D polar feature. A typical flow diagram of this approach is shown in Fig. 3.22.

Another method called *exponential MHI* (eMHI) is proposed that can update instantly the motion history of each pixel in the scene with exponential weights without explicitly specifying the exact duration of a movement [739]. The eMHI uses an exponential time update process to adjust the recency of motion at each pixel location. The eMHI can be produced according to the following equation,

$$eMHI(x, y, t) = M(x, y, t) + eMHI(x, y, t - 1).\alpha \qquad (3.39)$$

where,
α = the energy update rate $(0 < \alpha < 1)$. It is an important parameter for a good spatio-temporal representation. If the value is large, the accumulated motion energy of a pixel will decrease slowly and the produced template will have long trail of motion information; and vice-versa.
$M(x, y, t)$ can be computed from,

$$M(x, y, t) = \begin{cases} T_{energy} & \text{if } D(x, y, t) = 1 \\ 0 & \text{otherwise} \end{cases} \qquad (3.40)$$

where, T_{energy} is a predetermined energy constant (e.g., a typical value is 30). It is added to each foreground pixel. In this approach,

- For a foreground pixel, the energy of a pixel is increased and accumulated, if it remains as a foreground point. This is contrary to the MHI method where pixel values remain the same with maximum value for a foreground that remains as a foreground point.
- When it becomes a background point, the energy of the pixel value decays exponentially.

3.4.2 View-Invariant MHI Representations

In this subsection, we present 3D or view-invariant approaches that are developed at the top of the MHI.

Motion History Volume (MHV) is proposed by Weinland et al. [279, 531], which is considered as a 3D extension of the 2D MHI. It is developed on visual hull for viewpoint-independent action recognition. Visual hulls present several advantages, for example: they are easy to compute and they yield robust 3D representations. In the MHV approach, image pixels are replaced with voxels, and the standard image differencing function $D(x, y, t)$ is substituted with the space occupancy function $D(x, y, z, t)$, which is estimated using silhouettes and thus, corresponds to a visual hull [531]. Voxel values in the MHV at time t are defined as:

$$MHV_\tau(x, y, z, t) = \begin{cases} \tau & \text{if } D(x, y, z, t)) = 1 \\ \max(0, MHV_\tau(x, y, z, t - 1) - 1) & \text{otherwise} \end{cases}$$
$$(3.41)$$

It is assumed that the templates to be normalized and segmented with respect to the duration of an action,

$$MHV(x, y, z) = MHV_{\tau=t_{max}-t_{min}(x,y,z,t_{max})}/(t_{max} - t_{min}) \qquad (3.42)$$

where, t_{max} and t_{min} are the end time and start time of an action. Though it offers an alternative to action recognition with multiple cameras, additional computational cost due to calibration, synchronization of multiple cameras, and parallel background subtraction are challenging areas for the method [328]. In this case, classification is done using Mahalanobis distance and PCA; as well as using a combination of PCA and Linear Discriminant Analysis (LDA). Turaga et al. [38] use the view-invariant representations and features of [531]. They use the $16 \times 16 \times 16$ circular FFT features proposed by [531].

Another 3D MHI model is proposed by Shin et al. [276] called *3D Motion History Model* (3D-MHM). They address the following issues of gesture/action recognition namely,

- Camera view-invariance issue: In view-based methods, data for each viewpoint is required, which is ineffective and ambiguous in recognizing gestures [502]. They exploit the view-based MHI method to introduce a new view-invariant method. The camera view problem is very difficult in the environment of single directional camera (e.g., monocular or stereo camera) [276]. By utilizing the 3D-MHM with disparity information, they solve this constraint.
- Variable duration of a gesture: In order to address the duration problem that comes from the variation of gesture velocity at every performing time, they introduce a concept called *Dynamic History Buffering* (DHB). The DHB can improve the variable duration problem using magnitude of motion.
- The 3D-MHM improves the reliability of gesture recognition and the scalability of system.

They implement a real-time system and perform gesture recognition experiments. The system using 3D-MHM achieves better results of recognition than using only 2D motion information [276].

In the similar fashion, [276, 502] propose the *Volume Motion Template* (VMT) representation for gesture recognition, based on a stereo camera. They extract silhouette images using background subtraction with disparity maps. Here, motion orientation is determined with 3D motion information. The projection of a VMT at the optimal virtual viewpoint can be obtained by motion orientation [502]. This method is not only independent of variations of viewpoints, but also can represent depth motion to some extent. Their experiments demonstrate that this view-invariant representation can perform well, using ten gesture sequences which include parallel motion in an optical axis. However, in another extension by this group, they introduce *Projected Motion Template* (PMT). The PMT is generated by projecting the VMT into a 2D plane that is orthogonal to an optimal virtual viewpoint where the optimal virtual viewpoint is a viewpoint from which an action can be described in greatest detail, in 2D space [40]. The problem of variation of action speed is also solved by their temporal normalization method. In this case, the term *Volume Motion* (VM) does not imply an *actual* 3D volume, but a *virtual* volume of motion which is reconstructed from a pair of images by a stereo camera. We can generate the Volume Motion Template VMT_t based on the following steps according to [40],

- Extraction of silhouette foreground images and disparity maps, using the correspondence of stereo input images.
- Calculation of volume object, O_t at time t, in 3D space, using the silhouette image and the disparity map. The O_t,

$$O_t(x, y, z) = \begin{cases} 1 & \text{if } S_t(x, y)) = 1 \text{ and } Z_t(x, y) = z \\ 0 & \text{otherwise} \end{cases} \quad (3.43)$$

where,
S_t: Binary silhouette image.
Z_t: Its disparity map.

- Calculation of the motion difference (i.e., the difference of two consecutive volume objects), $\rho_t(x, y, z) = \|O_t(x, y, z) - O_{t-1}(x, y, z)\|$, and the magnitude of motion, μ_t, between two consecutive volume objects in motion sequence.
- Construction of the VMT_t, by adding new motion, ρ_t, and attenuating intensity of previous motion information with the magnitude of motion. Hence, the VMT_t at time t,

$$VMT_t(x, y, z) = \begin{cases} I_{max} & \text{if } \rho_t(x, y, z) = 1 \\ max(0, V_{t-1}(x, y, z) - \eta\mu_t) & \text{otherwise} \end{cases} \quad (3.44)$$

where,
I_{max}: Maximum intensity. For a grayscale image, $I_{max} = 255$.
η: Attenuating constant that controls the amount of disappearance of the motion history information.
μ_t: Magnitude of motion. Motion history information disappearance rate is reduced in proportion to this parameter μ_t.

The attenuating constant can be achieved by,

$$\eta = \frac{1}{N} \sum_{i=1}^{N} \frac{I_{max} - 1}{\sum_{t=1}^{T_i} \mu_t} \quad (3.45)$$

where,
N: Number of training data.
T_i: Length of ith training data.

Afterwards, normalization of the VMT is done in both spatial and temporal domains. The *Projected Motion Template* (PMT) is generated from the VMT and

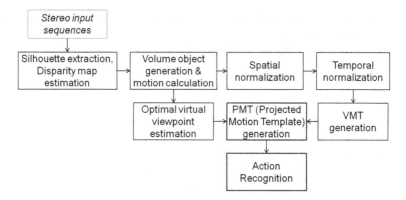

Fig. 3.23 A flow diagram of the Volume Motion Template (VMT) method

information of motion orientation. The PMT is used for recognition. Figure 3.23 shows a flow diagram of this method.

In the similar tone, with the added information of position of body limbs, Canton-Ferrer et al. [280, 509] develop a method called *Motion History Volume* (MHV) as a 3D-MHI and *Motion Energy Volume* (MEV) as a 3D-MEI template. To extract a set of features describing the body of a person that performs an action, a geometrical configuration of human body must be considered. Let's consider an ellipsoid model as a set of parameters, $\eta = (c, R, s)$. In this ellipsoid modeling of a human body candidate, c: Centroid of the body; R: Rotation along each axis centered on c; s: Length of each axis.

After obtaining the set of voxels $\Omega(x, y, z, t)$ describing a given person, we need to fit an ellipsoid shell to model it. The time consistency of η parameters is achieved by using a Kalman Filter. Once these three parameters are computed, a simple body part classification is derived, where each voxel is labeled as one of right or left arm and right or left leg. These data are used for classification of an action jointly with motion information [509].

A typical system overview is shown in Fig. 3.24. Apart from classifying actions, it is used to detect unusual behavior [281].

Another 3D-MHI representation, called the *Volumetric Motion History Image* (VMHI) is proposed by [291, 328]. The VMHI can be computed by the following equation based on binary silhouette images,

$$VMHI(x, y, \kappa) = \begin{cases} S(x, y, \kappa) \triangledown S(x, y, \kappa + 1) & \text{if } \psi S(x, y, \kappa) \neq \psi S(x, y, \kappa + 1) \\ 1 & \text{otherwise} \end{cases}$$

(3.46)

where,
$S(x, y, \kappa)$: Silhouette images ($\kappa = 1 \cdots N$).
$\psi S(x, y, \kappa)$: One pixel thick contour of the binary silhouette in frame κ.
Δ: Symmetric difference operator.

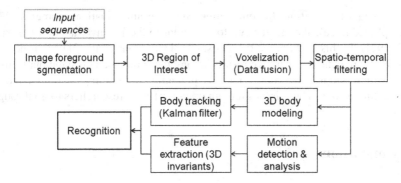

Fig. 3.24   A typical system overview of the Motion History Volume (MHV) method

κ: It encodes discrete temporal information.

Note that every slice in the VMHI representation is established on the integration of [328],

- the motion occurred within an adjacent frames—captured with the symmetric difference operator Δ between two adjacent binary silhouettes, and
- the spatial occupancy—captured with the binary contour $\psi S(x, y, \kappa)$ comparison.

In this approach, the temporal window τ is not necessary, unlike to the basic MHI or related approaches, where in the later cases, the τ is determined either empirically, or with an exhaustive research of the best correlation match between the template to be classified and a reference template [328]. They claim that the VMHI representation can overcome some constraints of the MHI method, e.g.,

- Motion self-occlusion due to overwriting: The VMHI can detect an occurrence of motion irregularity in two sequences and it can discriminate between any two motion irregularities [291].
- Subject-dependent motion speed: The computation of VMHI models for normal and abnormal motions without attempting to normalize the models for a direct inter-model comparison.
- Variable length of the action sequences: The VMHI representation can encode the temporal information along the z coordinate, which is a suitable solution for both long and short sequences [328].
- Motion periodicity: Due to the overwriting problem of the MHI method, it cannot perform well with periodic motions. However, the VMHI method can work with periodic motion.

The VMHI can be used for detecting the fundamental period of motion by searching for pairs of similar slice sequences in the VMHI model separated by a minimum number of frames [328].

Davis [277, 511] develop a system by concentrating at the problem of combining MHIs from multiple views (e.g., eight different views [277]) to perform view-invariant recognition. In some cases, 3D invariant statistical moments [278] are employed to calculate feature vectors (similar to the Hu invariants for the basic MHI [492]). In this section, we present some 3D versions of the 2D MHI method, however, there is no comparative results among these methods on same platform to justify which one is better and to identify potential shortcomings and application-specific dimensions. These issues remain open for future researchers to go through.

3.5 Conclusion

In this chapter, we present a tutorial of the Motion History Image and the Motion Energy Image templates for action or gesture or gait recognition and motion analysis. Various applications are presented, which are based on the MHI/MEI or its variants. We also present variants of the MHI/MEI representations in 2D and in 3D domains. It is noticeable that this representation has been very widely exploited and upgraded by a good number of researchers. However, more extensive researches are required to overcome some of the constraints of the MHI representation. It is also necessary to compare some of the important variants on a single platform with varieties of datasets to know the suitability of these approaches.

The MHI and its developments still cannot work with situations where multiple moving objects (e.g., persons, vehicles) in a scene. It cannot isolate moving objects easily. It is recommended that some sorts of tracking algorithms can be incorporated. Though there are various other approaches for motion representations and method-ologies for action recognition, the MHI and the MEI pair and the developments at the top of these representations still remain valid and attractive by many researchers for more than a decade now—mainly due to its simple computation and efficient repre-sentation. Fusing other features and incorporating probabilistic approaches will lead more applications at the top of the MHI representation.

Chapter 4
Action Datasets and MHI

Abstract There are a number of benchmark datasets for action, activity, gesture, and gait recognition. In this chapter, we present mainly those which are used to evaluate the MHI or its variants.

4.1 Various Datasets

There are a good number of datasets for various purposes. Although the dimensions and perspective vary from one to other, these datasets become known to the community. However, for the MHI, only few of those are exploited. In this section, we mention the names of various datasets. For detailed explanation on these, one may read the Chap. 6 from [36]. Various datasets are,

- KTH dataset [651]
- Weizmann dataset [601]
- INRIA IXMAS dataset [531]
- CASIA action dataset [131, 133]
- UMD dataset [103]
- ICS Action database [137]
- Korea University Gesture (KUG) database [136, 262]
- Wearable Action Recognition Database (WARD) [135]
- Biological Motion Library (BML) [130]
- HDM05 (Hochschule der Medien) Motion Capture database [129]
- Cambridge Gesture dataset [636]
- Naval Air Training and Operating Procedures Standardization (NATOPS) dataset [128]
- Keck gesture dataset [640]
- YouTube dataset [126]
- YouTube Video dataset [124]
- Hollywood2 Human Action (HOHA) dataset [660]

Md. A. R. Ahad, *Motion History Images for Action Recognition and Understanding*,
SpringerBriefs in Computer Science, DOI: 10.1007/978-1-4471-4730-5_4,
© Md. Atiqur Rahman Ahad 2013

- UCF sport action dataset [445]
- Soccer dataset [493]
- Figure-skating dataset—Caltech dataset [176]
- ADL—Assisted Daily Living dataset [139]
- Kisses/Slaps dataset [445]
- UIUC action dataset [104]
- Still image action dataset [172, 173]
- Nursing-home dataset [169]
- Collective Activity dataset [20]
- Coffee and Cigarettes dataset [150]
- People Playing Musical Instrument (PPMI) [175]
- DARPA's Mind's Eye Program [18]
- VIRAT video dataset [125]
- UMN Dataset: Unusual Crowd Activity [165]
- Web dataset [165, 166]
- HumanEva-I/II dataset [108]
- Interaction Dataset for *High-level Human Interaction Recognition Challenge* [19]
- Aerial-view for *Aerial View Activity Classification Challenge* [17]
- Wide-area Activity for *Wide-Area Activity Search and Recognition Challenge* [16]
- Dynamic Hand Posture database [46]
- Humanid Gait Challenge dataset [265]
- TREC Video Retrieval Evaluation: TRECVID [15]
- ChaLearn Gesture Challenge dataset [14]
- MSR Action Dataset of 63 actions [114]
- CMU motion capture database [13]
- Human Motion Database (HMD) at University of Texas at Arlington [123]
- Interactive Emotional Dyadic MoCo (IEMOCAP) database [122]
- Multi-camera Human Action Video dataset [121]
- Manually Annotated Silhouette Data from the MuHAVi dataset [121]
- Virtual Human Action Silhouette (ViHASi) dataset [119, 120, 324]
- POETICON Enacted Scenario Corpus [118]
- TMU Kitchen dataset [117]
- Carnegie Mellon University Multimodal Activity (CMUMMAC) database [116]
- i3DPost Multi-view dataset [115]
- CHIL 2007 Evaluation dataset [113]
- OpenDoor and SitDown-StandUp dataset [112]
- Several databases by Visual Geometry Gr. [111]
- Yilmaz and Shah's dataset [110]
- PETS benchmark dataset—e.g., PETS2006, PETS2007 [109]

Fig. 4.1 Some sample images for KTH dataset. Six actions are sequentially presented from Column1 through Column6 as walking, jogging, running, boxing, hand waving, and hand clapping

4.2 Datasets Employed in MHI

From the above enlisted datasets, only few datasets are tried with the MHI method and its variants. The question may arise—why! In fact, no single method on action recognition is tried with many datasets. Most of the approaches are mainly used by the originators or their groups and in a very few cases, by others. In this regard, the MHI gets much more attention and is explored in various datasets. Apart from the following datasets, it is experimented under various datasets developed by the authors, which are not open for others to use and compare. Therefore, we explore here only the publicly available and well-known datasets that are used in the MHI or its variants.

4.2.1 KTH Dataset

It is the most well-known and compared dataset! The KTH dataset is developed by [651] where only six different actions from a single person are taken by using a single camera. There is a slight camera movement in terms of panning and slight movement—but overall it is a difficult dataset. It has both indoor and outdoor actions of walking, running, jogging, boxing, hand waving, and hand clapping taken from 25 subjects. It has variability in terms of illumination, heights, clothing, directions of motions, presence of shadows, poor lighting, indoor-outdoor, panning of camera, camera movement, varied image depth, and so on. These are taken in four sets.

Figure 4.1 shows some sample frames of this dataset. The most difficult part of this dataset is the walking versus jogging versus running actions—as they overlap more than other actions. Some comparative recognition results are presented in Table 4.1.

Fig. 4.2 Some sample images for Weizmann dataset. Actions are (in *top-row*) run, gallop sideways, skip, jump forward on two legs, jumping in one place on two legs, (in *bottom-row*) bend, jumping jack, walk, waving one hand, and waving both hands

Table 4.1 Average action recognition rate by various methods in KTH dataset

Recognition approach	Average recognition rate (in %)
[60]	97.40
[632]	97.00
[642]	97.00
[146]	95.10
[636]	95.00
[637]	94.50
[140]	94.50
[638]	91.80
[658]	91.40
[452]	90.50
[649]	89.30
[145]	87.70
[646]	86.60
[643]	81.50
[473]	80.99
[651]	71.72

4.2.2 Weizmann Dataset

This is another well-known dataset based on single subject from a static camera. The Weizmann dataset [601] has 90 low-resolution (180 × 144) videos from nine different subjects, for 10 action classes. These are bend, jumping jack, jump forward, jump in place, run, gallop sideways, skip, walk, wave one hand, and wave both hands. Compared to the KTH dataset, it is very simple, and hence widely exploited. Figure 4.2 presents few images for each action. Some recognition results are shown in Table 4.2.

Table 4.2   Average action recognition rate by various methods in Weizmann dataset

Recognition approach	Average recognition rate (in %)
[2]	100.00
[602]	99.61
[1]	98.8
[146]	97.50
[147]	95.33
[145]	94.74
[12]	94.7
[4]	94.40
[3]	72.8

Table 4.3   Average recognition rate for INRIA IXMAS multi-view action dataset

Recognition approach	Average recognition rate (in %)
[531]	93.3
[743]	75.3
[11]	91.11
[444]	80.6
[324]	77.27

4.2.3 IXMAS Dataset

Above two datasets are based on a single camera. The INRIA IXMAS multi-view action dataset is taken from five synchronized and calibrated cameras, and hence this dataset can be used for view-invariant approaches. The IXMAS dataset [531] has 11 actors, each performing 13 actions with three repetitions. The actions are check watch, cross arms, scratch head, sit down, get up, turn around, walk, wave, punch, kick, point, pick up, and throw. Figure 4.3 shows some frames of this dataset. Table 4.3 shows some results. However, [11] recognize the actions per camera basis and the average recognition results are—65.4, 70.0, 54.3, 66.0, and 33.6 % from camera 1 to 5.

4.2.4 CASIA Gait Database

There is a CASIA action database and CASIA gait database by the Institute of Automation, Chinese Academy of Sciences (CASIA). The CASIA action dataset is a collection of sequences of human activities captured by multi-camera in outdoor environment [131, 133]. Like the above datasets, it has a single person in view for each of the eight actions. Actions are conducted by 24 subjects. The actions are— walk, run, bend, jump, crouch, faint, wander, and punching a car. The dataset also has interactions of two persons for seven different situations. These are—rob, fight,

Fig. 4.3 Some sample images for INRIA IXMAS multi-view action dataset

Fig. 4.4 Some sample images for CASIA gait dataset. Last two frames are from CASIA dataset C
(*infra-red* dataset) and others are from set A and set B

follow, follow and gather, meet and part, meet and gather, overtake [132]. On the
other hand, in the CASIA gait database there are three different datasets: Dataset A,
Dataset B (multi-view dataset), and Dataset C (infrared dataset). Figure 4.4 shows
some sample images [131].

However, the CASIA gait dataset is an indoor gait database and comprises 124
subjects. For each subject, there are 10 walking sequences consisting of six normal
walking sequences where the subject does not carry a bag or wear a bulky coat
(CASIA set A), two carrying bag sequences (CASIA set B) and two wearing coat
sequences (CASIA set C) [5]. Each sequence contains multiple gait cycles. Of these
sets, set A is simpler than the other two sets. For set A, the result is 99.4 % using the
Gait Energy Image (GEI) [297] and 98.3 % using the Gait Entropy Image (GEnI)
[5]. This is shown in Table 4.4.

Table 4.4   Average recognition rate with CASIA dataset

Set	Recognition approach	Average recognition rate (in %)
CASIA set A	[297]	99.4
CASIA set A	[5]	98.3
CASIA set B	[297]	60.2
CASIA set B	[5]	80.1
CASIA set C	[297]	30.0
CASIA set C	[5]	33.5

Table 4.5   Some recognition rates with ViHASi dataset

Recognition approach	Average recognition rate (in %)
[119]	98.68
[324]	98.48
[12]	97.6

4.2.5   Virtual Human Action Silhouette (ViHASi) Dataset

The ViHASi—Virtual Human Action Silhouette Dataset is developed for the evaluation of silhouette-based action recognition methods and the evaluation of silhouette-based pose recovery methods [119, 120, 324]. Figure 4.5 shows some sample silhouettes from this dataset.

It consists of 20 action classes from nine actors and up to 40 synchronized perspective camera views. This dataset provides accurate silhouette images, which is usually extracted from raw video sequences, and hence if the silhouettes' extraction are erroneous—then the recognition method will not demonstrate the expected accurate results. Therefore, this dataset is the one to mitigate this problem. They achieve 98.68 % average recognition rate with this dataset. Some comparative recognition results are shown in Table 4.5. Note that these are not the exact rates because, different groups considered different combinations for camera settings, number of subjects, or actions. We put reasonably approximate recognition results in this table. However, using different combinations of cameras, actions, and subjects—the recognition results vary slightly.

4.2.6 CMU MoBo Dataset

The Carnegie Mellon University (CMU) Motion of Body (MoBo) Database [10] is a well-known dataset for gait analysis. It contains 25 individuals walking on a treadmill, for each of four gait types—slow walk, fast walk, ball walk, and inclined walk. The MoBo database is suitable for checking the performance of the shape variation cue compared to the previous shape-only cues. The number of walking cycles is large. The clustered-based Dominant Energy Image (DEI) [302] exploits

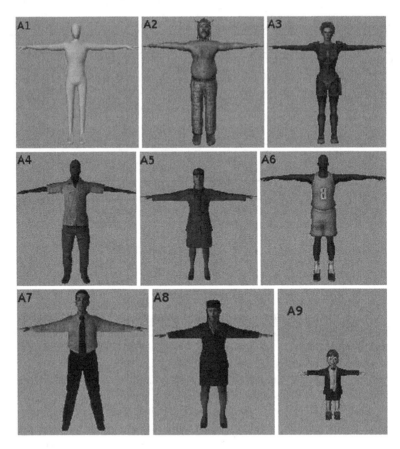

Fig. 4.5 Some sample silhouettes from ViHASi dataset. It demonstrates the diversity of this dataset

the CMU Mobo Gait Database and achieved 82 % recognition accuracy. With Gallery data versus Probe data—various combinations produce different results. Using SVB frieze, average recognition of 84.67 % is achieved for all combinations [9].

4.2.7 USF HumanID Dataset

The USF (University of South Florida) Human ID Gait Challenge Problem [6, 7, 8, 265, 740] consists of a large data set—about 1.2 TB of data related to 1870 sequences from 122 subjects spanning five covariates. The dataset consists of persons walking in elliptical paths in front of the camera(s). Each person walked multiple (≥ 5) circuits around an ellipse, out of which the last circuit forms the dataset. The five covariates for each person are,

- Two different shoe types (A and B)
- Two different carrying conditions (with or without a briefcase)

- On two different surface types (grass and concrete)
- From two different viewpoints (left or right) and
- Some at two different time instants

The baseline algorithm involves silhouette estimation by background subtraction and similarity computation by temporal correlation of the silhouettes. The instructions to get the gait data, the source code of the baseline algorithm, and scripts used to run the challenge experiment are available in there website.

4.2.8 Marcel's Dynamic Hand Poster and Gesture Dataset

A dynamic hand posture and gesture dataset is developed by Marcel [46]. The dataset consists of 15 video sequences for each of the four dynamic hand gestures, which are—Click, No, StopGraspOk, and Rotate. Reference [292] use the MHI with the Fisher Discriminant Analysis (FDA) in this dataset.

4.2.9 TRECVID Dataset

This dataset (TRECVID) is maintained by USA Government for over a decade. Video shot classification is done by considering *Edge Motion History Image* (EMHI) [311, 316]. They choose 60 min CNN video from the TRECVID'05 dataset to estimate all the GMMs in layer 1 and layer 2. Classification topics of video shots are based on the TRECVID'03 dataset, where randomly extracted 100 video shots are considered. Six different classes: indoor, outdoor, news person, news subject, sport, and weather are tested [316]. There is no video shot contains more than one topic. There is no training data and test data are extracted from the same video in each topic [316].

4.3 Conclusion

This chapter is about databases related to action, gesture, and gait recognition. All good datasets are mentioned here. We detail only those datasets that are exploited by the MHI and its variants. However, most of the methods exploit their own datasets and these are not available for researchers to explore and compare. And this chapter concludes this book.

References

1. Jhuang H, Serre T, Wolf L, Poggio T (2007) A biologically inspired system for action recognition. ICCV
2. Ikizler N, Duygulu P (2007) Human action recognition using distribution of oriented rectangular patches. Human motion ICCV
3. Niebles JC, Fei–Fei L (2007) A hierarchical model of shape and appearance for human action classification. IEEE CVPR
4. Thurau C, Hlavac V (2008) Pose primitive based human action recognition in videos or still images. IEEE CVPR
5. Bashir K, Xiang T, Gong S (2009) Gait recognition using gait entropy image. International Conference on Imaging for Crime Detection and Prevention
6. Sarkar S, Jonathon Phillips P, Liu Z, Robledo I, Grother P, Bowyer KW (2005) The human ID gait challenge problem: data sets, performance, and analysis. IEEE Trans Pattern Anal Mach Intell 27(2):162–177
7. Phillips PJ, Sarkar S, Robledo I, Grother P, Bowyer KW (2002) The gait identification challenge problem: data sets and baseline algorithm. International conference on, pattern recognition, pp 385–388
8. Phillips P, Sarkar S, Robledo I, Grother P, Bowyer K (2002) Baseline results for the challenge problem of Human ID using gait analysis. IEEE AFGR
9. Lee S, Liu Y, Collins R (2007) Shape variation-based frieze pattern for robust gait recognition
10. Gross R, Shi J (2001) The CMU motion of body (MoBo) database. Technical report CMU-RI-TR-01-18, robotics institute CMU
11. Weinland D, Boyer E, Ronfard R (2007) Action recognition from arbitrary views using 3D exemplars. ICCV
12. Marin-Jimenez M, Blanca N, Mendoza M (2010) RBM-based silhouette encoding for human action modelling. ICPR
13. CMU Motion Capture Database. http://mocap.cs.cmu.edu
14. ChaLearn Gesture Challenge Dataset. http://gesture.chalearn.org
15. TREC Video Retrieval Evaluation: TRECVID. http://trecvid.nist.gov
16. UT-wide-area DB. http://cvrc.ece.utexas.edu/SDHA2010/Wide_Area_Activity.html
17. UT-Aerial-view DB. http://cvrc.ece.utexas.edu/SDHA2010/Aerial_View_Activity.html
18. DARPA's Minds Eye. http://www.darpa.mil/Our_Work/I2O/Programs/Minds_Eye.aspx
19. UT-Interaction DB. http://cvrc.ece.utexas.edu/SDHA2010/Human_Interaction.html
20. Collective Database. http://www.eecs.umich.edu/vision/activity-dataset.html

21. Shen Y, Foroosh H (2009) View-invariant action recognition from point triplets. IEEE transactions PAMI
22. Souvenir R, Babbs J (2008) Learning the viewpoint manifold for action recognition. IEEE Conference, CVPR
23. Parameswaran V, Chellappa R (2003) View invariants for human action recognition. IEEE Conference, CVPR
24. Gong D, Medioni G (2011) Dynamic manifold warping for view invariant action recognition. ICCV
25. Yuedong Y, Aimin H, Qinping Z (2008) View-Invariant action recognition using interest points. ACM MIR
26. Xia L, Chen C, Aggarwal J (2012) View invariant human action recognition using histograms of 3D joints. understanding, modeling, capture and animation, ECCV workshop on human motion
27. Noguchi, Yanai K (2010) A SURF-based spatio-temporal feature for feature- fusion-based action recognition. understanding, modeling, capture and animation, ECCV workshop on human motion
28. Guerra-Filho G, Aloimonos Y (2007) A language for human action. Computer 40:42–51
29. Green R, Guan L (2004) Quantifying and recognizing human movement patterns from monocular video images—part i: a new framework for modeling human motion. IEEE Trans Circuits Syst Video Techn 14:179–190
30. Kulkarni K, Boyer E, Horaud R, Kale A (2010) An unsupervised framework for action recognition using actemes. Asian conference on computer vision
31. Bobick A (1987) Movement, activity, and action: the role of knowledge in the perception of motion. Philos Trans Royal Soc Lond 352:1257–1265
32. Gonzalez J, Varona J, Roca F, Villanueva J (2002) aSpaces: action spaces for recognition and synthesis of human actions. Internatinal workshop on articulated motion and deformable objects
33. Jenkins O, Mataric M (2002) Automated modularization of human motion into actions and behaviors. Technical report CRES-02-002, enter for robotics and embedded systems, University of Southern California
34. Nagel H (1988) From image sequences towards conceptual descriptions. Image Vision Comput 6(2):59–74
35. Kruger V, Kragic D, Ude A, Geib C The meaning of action—a review on action recognition and mapping. IEEE J Select Top Signal Proc
36. Ahad AR Md (2011) Computer vision and action recognition. Atlantic Press, Amsterdam, Paris
37. Holte M, Tran C, Trivedi M, Moeslund T (2011) Human 3D pose estimation and activity recognition from multi-view videos: comparative explorations of recent developments. IEEE J Select Top Signal Proc
38. Turaga P, Veeraraghavan A, Chellappa R (2008) Statistical analysis on stiefel and grassmann manifolds with applications in computer vision. IEEE conference on computer vision and pattern recognition
39. Naiel M, Abdelwahab M, El-Saban M (2011) Multi-view human action recognition system employing 2DPCA. IEEE workshop on applications of computer vision, pp 270–275
40. Roh M, Shin H, Lee S (2010) View-independent human action recognition with volume motion template on single stereo camera. Pattern Recognit Lett 31:639–647
41. Lee C, Chuang C, Hsieh J, Wu M, Fan K (2011) Frame difference history image for gait recognition. International conference on machine learning and, cybernetics, pp 1785–1788
42. Chen C, Liang J, Zhao H, Hu H, Tian J (2009) Frame difference energy image for gait recognition with incomplete silhouettes. Pattern Recognit Lett 30:977–984
43. Xue Z, Ming D, Song W, Wan B, Jin S (2010) Infrared gait recognition based on wavelet transform and support vector machine. Pattern Recognition, 43:2904–2910

44. Liu L, Zheng N, Xiong L (2009) Silhouette quality quantification for gait sequence analysis and recognition. Signal Proc 89:1417–1427
45. Zhou X, Bhanu B (2007) Integrating face and gait for human recognition at a distance in Video. IEEE Trans SMS—part B. Cybernetics 37(5):353–359
46. Marcel S. Dynamic Hand Posture Database. http://www-prima.inrialpes.fr/FGnet/data/10-Gesture/dhp_marcel.tar.gz
47. Yao A, Gall J, Gool L (2012) Coupled action recognition and pose estimation from multiple views. IJCV, 100(1):16–37
48. Lam T, Lee R, Zhang D (2007) Human gait recognition by the fusion of motion and static spatio-temporal templates. Pattern Recognit 40:2563–2573
49. Triggs B (1998) Autocalibration from planar scenes. European conference on computer vision, pp 89–105
50. Stein G (1995) Accurate internal camera calibration using rotation, with analysis of sources of error. international conference on computer vision, pp 230–236
51. Caprile B, Torre V (1990) Using vanishing points for camera calibration. Intl J Compur Vis 4(2):127–140
52. Liebowitz D, Zisserman A (1998) Metric rectification for perspective images of planes. In Proceeding IEEE conference on computer vision and pattern recognition, pp 482–488, Santa Barbara, California
53. Hartley RI (1994) An algorithm for self calibration from several views. In Proceeding IEEE conference on computer vision and, pattern recognition, pp 908–912
54. Luong Q-T, Faugeras O (1997) Self-calibration of a moving camera from point correspondences and fundamental matrices. Int J Comp Vis 22(3):261–289
55. Maybank SJ, Faugeras OD (1992) A theory of selfcalibration of a moving camera. Int J Comp Vis 8(2):123–152
56. Tsai R (1987) A versatile camera calibration technique for high-accuracy 3D machine vision metrology using off-the-shelf tv cameras and lenses. IEEE J Robotics Autom 3(4):323–344
57. Zhang Z (1999) Flexible camera calibration by viewing a plane from unknown orientations, IEEE
58. Blake R, Shiffrar M (2007) Perception of human motion. Ann Rev Psychol 58(1):47–73
59. Castrodad A, Sapiro G (2012) Sparse modeling of human actions from motion imagery. IJCV 100(1):1–15
60. Guo K, Ishwar P, Konrad J (2010) Action recognition using sparse representation on covariance manifolds of optical flow. IEEE international conference on advanced video and signal based surveillance
61. Ahad M, Tan J, Kim H, Ishikawa S (2011) Approaches for global-based action representations for games and action understanding. IEEE Automatic Face and Gesture Recognition, pp 753–758
62. Rosten E, Drummond T (2005) Fusing points and lines for high performance tracking. International conference on computer vision
63. Chen C, Aggarwal J (2009) Recognizing human action from a far field of view. IEEE workshop on motion and video computing
64. Willamowski J, Arregui D, Csurka G, Dance C, Fan L (2004) Categorizing nine visual classes using local appearance descriptors. IWLAVS
65. Matikainen P, Hebert M, Sukthankar R (2009) Trajectons: action recognition through the motion analysis of tracked features. VOEC workshop
66. Bosch A, Zisserman A, Munoz X (2007) Image classification using random forests and ferns. International conference on computer vision
67. Sun Z, Tan T (2009) Ordinal measures for iris recognition. IEEE transaction pattern analysis and machine intelligence
68. Fawcett T (2006) An introduction to ROC analysis. Pattern Recognit Lett 27:861–874

69. Wang X, Tang X (2004) Random sampling LDA for face recognition. IEEE Computer Vision and Pattern Recognition
70. Mallapragada P, Rong J, Jain A, Yi L (2009) SemiBoost: boosting for semi-supervised learning. IEEE transaction pattern analysis and machine intelligence
71. Pavlidis I, Morellas V, Tsiamyrtzis V, Harp S (2001) Urban surveillance systems: from the laboratory to the commercial world. Proceedings of the IEEE pp 1478–1497
72. Lo B, Velastin S (2001) Automatic congestion detection system for underground platforms. International symposium on intell. multimedia, video and speech processing pp 158–161
73. Cucchiara R, Grana C, Piccardi M, Prati A (2003) Detecting moving objects, ghosts and shadows in video streams. IEEE Trans Pattern Anal Mach Intell 25(10):1337–1342
74. Han B, Comaniciu D, Davis L (2004) Sequential kernel density approximation through mode propagation: applications to background modeling. Asian conference on computer vision
75. Oliver N, Rosario B, Pentland A (2000) A Bayesian computer vision system for modeling human interactions. IEEE Trans Pattern Anal Mach Intell 22(8):831–843
76. Liu X (2009) Discriminative face alignment. IEEE trans, Pattern analysis and machine intelligence
77. Hsu C, Lin C (2002) A comparison of methods for multiclass, support vector machines. IEEE Trans Neural Netw 13(2):415–425
78. Vapnik V (1998) Statistical learning theory. Wiley Publications, New York
79. Gleicher M (1999) Animation from observation: motion capture and motion editing. Comp Graph 33:51–54
80. Horn B (2000) Tsai's camera calibration method revisited. http://people.csail.mit.edu/bkph/articles/Tsai_Revisited.pdf
81. Abdel-Aziz Y, Karara H (1971) Direct linear transformation from comparator coordinates into object space coordinates in close-range photogrammetry. Symposium on close-range photogrammetry, pp 1–18
82. Hartley R, Zisserman A (2004) Multiple view geometry in computer vision. Cambridge University Press, Cambridge
83. Chum O, Matas J (2005) Matching with PROSAC—progressive sample consensus. IEEE Comp Vis Pattern Recognit 1:220–226
84. Nister D (2003) Preemptive RANSAC for live structure and motion estimation. International Conference on Computer Vision 1
85. Matas J, Chum O, Urba M, Pajdla T (2002) Robust wide baseline stereo from maximally stable extremal regions. British Machine Vision Conference
86. Belongie S, Malik J (2000) Matching with shape contexts. IEEE workshop on contentbased access of image and video libraries
87. Viola P, Jones M (2001) Rapid object detection using boosted cascade of simple features. IEEE computer vision and pattern recognition
88. Piccardi M (2004) Background subtraction techniques: a review. IEEE international conference on systems, Man and cybernetics
89. Bouwmans T (2009) Subspace learning for background modeling: a survey. Recent Pat Comp Sci 2(3):223–234
90. Elhabian S, El-Sayed E, Ahmed S (2008) Moving object detection in spatial domain using background removal techniques-state-of-art. Recent patents on computer science
91. Sarfraz S, Hellwich O (2008) Head pose estimation in face recognition across pose scenarios. International conference on computer vision theory and applications, pp 235–242
92. Kim S, Yoon K, Kweon I (2006) Object recognition using a generalized robust invariant feature and Gestalt's law of proximity and similarity. IEEE computer vision and pattern recognition workshop
93. Lazebnik S, Schmid C, Ponce J (2004) Semi-local affine parts for object recognition. British machine vision conference

94. Lowe D (1999) Object recognition from local scale-invariant features. Int Conf Comp Vis 2:1150–1157 (L. 2007)
95. Deng H, Zhang W, Mortensen E, Dietterich T, Shapiro L (2007) Principal curvature-based region detector for object recognition. IEEE computer vision and pattern recognition
96. Wang H, Brady M (1995) Real-time corner detection algorithm for motion estimation. Image Vis Comput 13(9):695–703
97. Mikolajczyk K, Schmid C (2004) Scale and affine invariant interest point detectors. Int J Comp Vis 60(1):63–86
98. Harris C, Stephens M (1988) A combined corner and edge detector. 4th alvey vision conference, pp 147–151
99. Trajkovic M, Hedley M (1998) Fast corner detection. Image Vis Comput 16(2):75–87
100. Smith S, Brady J (1997) SUSAN—a new approach to low level image processing. Int J Comp Vis 23:45–78
101. Sridhar M, Cohn A, Hogg D (2010) Discovering an event taxonomy from video using qualitative spatio-temporal graphs. European conference on artificial intelligence
102. Guan P, Freifeld O, Black M (2010) A 2D human body model dressed in eigen clothing. European conference on computer vision
103. Veeraraghavan A, Chellappa R, Roy-Chowdhury A (2006) The function space of an activity. IEEE computer vision and pattern recognition
104. Tran D, Sorokin A (2008) Human activity recognition with metric learning. European conference on computer vision
105. Thioux M, Gazzola V, Keyesers C (2008) Action understanding: how, what and why. Current biology 18(10):171–179
106. Yamane K, Nakamura Y (2010) Human motion database with a binary tree and node transition graphs. J Auton Robots 29(2):502–528
107. Ahad M, Tan J, Kim H, Ishikawa S (2011) Action dataset—a survey. SICE annual conference
108. Sigal L, Balan A, Black M (2010) HumanEva: synchronized video and motion capture dataset and baseline algorithm for evaluation of articulated human motion. Int J Comp Vis 87:1–2
109. PETS (2007) Workshops on Performance Evaluation of Tracking & Surveillance (PETS). http://www.cvg.rdg.ac.uk/PETS2007/data.html
110. Yilmaz A, Shah M (2005) Recognizing human actions in videos acquired by uncalibrated moving cameras. International conference on computer vision
111. Patron-Perez A, Marszalek M, Zisserman A, Reid I (2010) High five: recognising human interactions in TV shows. British machine vision conference
112. Duchenne O, Laptev I, Sivic J, Bach F, Ponce J (2009) Automatic annotation of human actions in video international conference on computer vision
113. Burger S (2008) The CHIL RT07 evaluation data. Multimodal technologies for perception of humans
114. MSR action dataset. http://research.microsoft.com/en-us/um/people/zliu/actionrecorsrc/default.htm
115. Gkalelis N, Kim H, Hilton A, Nikolaidis N, Pitas I (2009) The i3DPost multi-view and 3D human action/interaction database. Conference on visual media production
116. Hodgins F, Macey J (2009) Guide to the Carnegie Mellon University multimodal activity (cmu-mmac), database. CMU-RI-TR-08-22
117. Tenorth M, Bandouch J, Beetz M (2009) The TUM kitchen data set of everyday manipulation activities for motion tracking and action recognition. IEEE international workshop on tracking humans for the evaluation of their motion in image sequences with international conference on computer vision
118. Wallraven C, Schultze M, Mohler B, Vatakis A, Pastra K (2011) The POETICON enacted scenario corpus—a tool for human and computational experiments on action understanding. IEEE automatic face and gesture recognition. http://poeticoncorpus.kyb.mpg.de

119. Ragheb H, Velastin S, Remagnino P, Ellis T (2008) ViHASi: virtual human action silhouette data for the performance evaluation of silhouette-based action recognition methods workshop on activity monitoring by multi-camera surveillance systems

120. ViHASi Virtual Human Action Silhouette (ViHASi) database. http://dipersec.king.ac.uk/VIHASI/

121. MuHAVi. http://dipersec.king.ac.uk/MuHAVi-MAS

122. Busso C, Bulut M, Lee C, Kazemzadeh A, Mower E, Kim S, Chang J, Lee S, Narayanan S (2008) IEMOCAP: interactive emotional dyadic motion capture database. Lang Res Eval 42(4):335–359

123. Guerra-Filho G, Biswas A (2011) The human motion database: a cognitive and parametric sampling of human motion. IEEE automatic face and gesture recognition

124. Niebles J, Han B, Ferencz B, Fei-Fei L (2008) Extracting moving people from internet videos. European conference on computer vision

125. VIRAT (2011) VIRAT database. http://www.viratdata.org

126. Liu J, Luo J, Shah M (2009) Recognizing realistic actions from videos "in the wild". IEEE computer vision and pattern recognition

127. Keck gesture database. http://www.umiacs.umd.edu/~shivnaga/supplmat_ActionRec BallisticDyn_CVPR08/action_rec_using_ballistic_dynamics.html#gesture_rec

128. Song Y, Demirdjian D, Davis R (2011) Tracking body and hands for gesture recognition: NATOPS aircraft handling signals database. IEEE Autom Face Gesture Recognit

129. Muller M, Ryder T, Clausen M, Eberhardt B, Kruger B, Weber A (2007) Documentation: Mocap database HDM05. Universitat Bonn, Technical report CG-2007-2

130. Ma Y, Paterson H, Pollick F (2006) A motion capture library for the study of identity, gender, and emotion perception from biological motion. Behav Res Methods 38:134–141

131. CASIA Database. http://www.cbsr.ia.ac.cn/english/Action%20Databases%20EN.asp

132. Zhang Z, Huang K, Tan T (2008) Multi-thread parsing for recognizing complex events in videos. European conference on computer vision

133. Wang Y, Huang K, Ta T (2007) Human activity recognition based on R transform. IEEE computer vision and pattern recognition

134. WAR. http://www.eecs.berkeley.edu/

135. Yang A, Jarafi R, Kuryloski P, Iyengar S, Sastry S, Bajcsy R (2008) Distributed segmentation and classification of human actions using a wearable motion sensor network. Workshop on human communicative behavior analysis with computer vision and pattern recognition

136. Hwang B, Kim S, Lee S (2006) A full-body gesture database for automatic gesture recognition. IEEE automatic face and gesture recognition

137. ICS Action Database, The University of Tokyo. http://www.ics.t.u-tokyo.ac.jp/action

138. Vasconcelos M, Vasconcelos N (2009) Natural image statistics and low-complexity feature selection. IEEE Trans Pattern Anal Mach Intell 31(2):228–244

139. Messing R, Pal C, Kautz H (2009) Activity recognition using the velocity histories of tracked keypoints. International conference on computer vision

140. Gilbert A, Illingworth J, Bowden R (2010) Action recognition using mined hierarchical compound features. IEEE trans, Pattern analysis and machine intelligence

141. Yaffet L, Wolf L (2009) Local trinary patterns for human action. International conference on computer vision

142. Raptis M, Soatto S (2010) Tracklet descriptors for action modeling and video analysis. European conference on computer vision

143. Bregonzio M, Li J, Gong S, Xiang T (2010) Discriminative topics modelling for action feature selection and recognition. British machine vision conference

144. Liu G, Zhang J, Wang W, McMillan L (2005) A system for analyzing and indexing human—motion databases. SIGMOD

145. Ali S, Shah M (2010) Human action recognition in videos using kinematic features and multiple instance learning. IEEE Trans Pattern Anal Mach Intell 32(2):288–303

146. Seo H, Milanfar P (2011) Action recognition from one example. IEEE trans, Pattern analysis and machine intelligence
147. Junejo I, Dexter E, Laptev I, Perez P (2011) View-independent action recognition from temporal self-similarities. IEEE Trans Pattern Anal Mach Intell 33:172–185
148. Satkin S, Hebert M (2010) Modeling the temporal extent of actions.European conference on computer vision
149. Schindler K, Van Gool L (2008) Action snippets: How many frames does human action recognition require. IEEE Comp Vis Pattern Recognit
150. Gaidon A, Harchaoui Z, Schmid C (2011) Actom sequence models for efficient action detection. IEEE computer vision and pattern recognition
151. Fischler M, Bolles R (1981) Random sample consensus: a paradigm for model fitting with applications to image analysis and automated cartography. Commun ACM 24(6):381–395
152. Chen Y, Dang X, Peng H, Bart H (2009) Outlier detection with the kernelized spatial depth function. IEEE trans, Pattern analysis and machine intelligence
153. Friedman J (1989) Regularized discriminant analysis. J Am Stat Assoc
154. Bensmail H, Celeux G (1996) Regularized Gaussian discriminant analysis through Eigenvalue decomposition. J Am Stat Assoc
155. Bouveyron C, Girard S, Schmid C (2007) High dimensional discriminant analysis. Communication in statistics, theory and methods
156. Tao D, Ji X, Wu X, Maybank S (2009) Geometric mean for subspace selection. IEEE trans, Pattern analysis and machine intelligence
157. Lolitkar R, Kothari R (2000) Fractional-step dimensionality reduction. IEEE trans, Pattern analysis and machine intelligence
158. Sanja F, Skocaj D, Leonardis A (2006) Combining reconstructive and discriminative subspace methods for robust classification and regression by subsampling. IEEE trans, Pattern analysis and machine intelligence
159. Kim J, Choi J, Yi J, Turk M (2005) Effective representation using ICA for face recognition robust to local distortion and partial occlusion. IEEE Trans Pattern Anal Mach Intell 27(12):1977–1981
160. Belhumeur P, Hesanha J, Kreigman D (1997) Eigenfaces vs Recognition using class specific linear projection. IEEE trans pattern analysis and machine intelligence, Fisherfaces
161. Li S, Hou X, Zhang H, Cheng Q (2001) Learning spatially localized, parts-based representation. IEEE computer vision and pattern recognition
162. Ho J, Yang M, Lim J, Lee K, Kriegman D (2003) Clustering appearances of objects under varying illumination conditions. IEEE computer vision and pattern recognition
163. Wright J, Yang A, Ganesh A, Sastry S, Ma Y (2009) Robust face recognition via sparse representation. IEEE trans, Pattern analysis and machine intelligence
164. Zhang X, Fan G (2010) Dual gait generative models for human motion estimation from a single camera. IEEE transaction on systems, man, and cybernetics, part B. Cybernetics 40(4):1034–1049
165. Mehran R, Oyama A, Shah M (2009) Abnormal crowd behavior detection using social force model. IEEE computer vision and pattern recognition
166. Web dataset, UCF Web Dataset. http://www.cs.ucf.edu/~ramin/?page_id=24#2. Experiments_on_Web_Dataset
167. Mehran R, Moore B, Shah M (2010) A streakline representation of flow in crowded scenes. European conference on computer vision
168. Niebles J, Wang H, Fei-Fei L (2006) Unsupervised learning of human action categories using spatial-temporal words. British machine vision conference
169. Lan T, Wang Y, Mori G, Robinovitc S (2010) Retrieving actions in group contexts. International workshop on sign gesture activity with European conference on computer vision
170. Lan T, Wang Y, Yang W, Mori G (2010) Beyond actions: Discriminative models for contextual group activities. Neural information processing systems (NIPS)

171. Lan T, Wang Y, Mori G (2011) Discriminative figure-centric models for joint action localization and recognition. International conference on computer vision

172. Ikizler N, Cinbis R, Pehlivan S, Duygulu P (2008) Recognizing actions from still images. International conference on pattern recognition

173. Ikizler N, Cinbis R, Sclaroff S (2009) Learning actions from the web. International conference on computer vision

174. Yang W, Wang Y, Mori G (2010) Recognizing human actions from still images with latent poses. IEEE Comp Vis Pattern Recognit

175. Yao B, Fei-Fei L (2010) A structured image representation for recognizing human and object interactions. IEEE computer vision and pattern recognition

176. Wang Y, Jiang H, Drew M, Li Z, Mori G (2008) Unsupervised discovery of action classes. IEEE computer vision and pattern recognition

177. Fanti C (2008) Towards automatic discovery of human movemes. PhD Thesis, California Institute of Technology. http://www.vision.caltech.edu/publications/phdthesis_fanti.pdf

178. Del Vecchio D, Murray R, Perona P (2002) Primitives for human motion: a dynamical approach. IFAC world congress on automatic control

179. Bregler C, Malik J (1997) Learning and recognizing human dynamics in video sequences. IEEE computer vision and, pattern recognition, pp 568–674

180. Goncalves L, Di Bernardo E, Perona P (1998) Reach out and touch space (motion learning). IEEE Automatic Face and Gesture Recognition, pp 234–239

181. Song Y, Goncalves L, Perona P (2001) Unsupervised learning of human motion models. Advances in neural information processing systems (NIPS)

182. Wang Y, Mori G (2011) Hidden part models for human action recognition: probabilistic vs. max-margin. IEEE Transaction on Pattern Analysis and Machine Intelligence

183. Choi W, Shahid K, Savarese S (2011) Learning context for collective activity recognition. IEEE computer vision and pattern recognition

184. Choi W, Shahid K, Savarese S (2009) What are they doing? Collective activity classification using spatio-temporal relationship among people. International workshop on visual surveillance (VSWS09) with international conference on computer vision

185. Murase H, Lindenbaum M (1995) Partial eigenvalue decomposition of large images using spatial temporal adaptive method. IEEE Trans Image Proc 4(5):622–629

186. Rahman M, Ishikawa S (2005) Human posture recognition: eigenspace tuning by mean eigenspace. Int J Image Graph 5(4):825–837

187. Viola P, Jones M (2000) Robust real-time object detection. IEEE workshop on statistical and computational theories of vision

188. Black M, Jepson A (1998) Eigen tracking: robust matching and tracking of articulated objects using view-based representation. Int J Comp Vis 26(1):63–84

189. Ohba K, Ikeuchi K (1997) Detectability, uniqueless and reliability of eigen windows for stable verifications of partially occluded objects. IEEE Trans Pattern Anal Mach Intell 9:1043–1047

190. Murase H, Nayar K (1995) Visual learning and recognition of 3-D objects from appearance. Int J Comp Vis 14:39–50

191. Li Z, Wang K, Li L, Wang F (2006) A review on vision-based pedestrian detection for intelligent vehicles. ICVES, pp 57–62

192. MIAC-JP. Ministry of Internal Affairs and Communications, JAPAN. http://www.stat.go.jp/english/data/nenkan/1431-26.htm

193. The World Bank. http://www.worldbank.org/html/fpd/transport/roads/safety.htm

194. Krotosky S, Trivedi M (2007) On color-, infrared-, and multimodal-stereo approaches to pedestrian detection. IEEE Trans ITS 8(4):619–629

195. Zhang Z, Faugeras O (1992) Three-dimensional motion computation and object segmentation in a long sequence of stereo frames. Int J Comp Vis 7:211–241

196. Chang Y, Aggarwal J (1991) 3D structure reconstruction from an ego motion sequence using statistical estimation and detection theory.Workshop on visual motion

197. Sethi I, Jain R (1987) Finding trajectories of feature points in a monocular image sequence. IEEE Trans Pattern Anal Mach Intell 9:56–73
198. Cui N, Weng J, Cohen P (1990) Extended structure and motion analysis from monocular image sequences. International conference on computer vision, pp 222–229
199. Weng J, Ahuja N, Huang T (1992) Matching two perspective views. IEEE Trans Pattern Anal Mach Intell 14:806–825
200. Tomasi C, Kanade T (1991) Detection and tracking of point features. Carnegie Mellon University, Technical report CMU-CS-91-132
201. Hager G, Belhumeur P (1996) Real-time tracking of image regions with changes in geometry and illumination. IEEE computer vision and, pattern recognition, pp 403–410
202. Tommasini T, Fusiello A, Trucco E, Roberto V (1998) Making good features track better. IEEE computer vision and pattern recognition
203. Shi J, Tomasi C (1994) Good features to track. IEEE computer vision and pattern recognition
204. Yao Y, Chellappa R (1995) Tracking a dynamic set of feature points. IEEE Trans Image Proc 4(10):1382–1395
205. Yao Y, Chellappa R (1994) Dynamic feature point tracking in an image sequence. IAPR Comp Vis Pattern Recognit 1:654–657
206. Naito Y, Okatani T, Deguchi K (2003) Comparison of the feature point tracking method in image sequences. SICE annual conference pp 1326–1331
207. Wang Y, Cao L, Huang W (2003) 3-D human motion estimation using regularization with 2-d feature point tracking. International conference on machine learning and, cybernetics pp 2931–2935
208. Borgefors G (1988) Hierarchical chamfer matching: a parametric edge matching algorithm. IEEE Trans Pattern Anal Mach Intell 10(6):849–865
209. Peterson L (2009) K-nearest neighbor. http://www.scholarpedia.org/article/K-nearest_neighbor 4:2
210. Weinberger K, Blitzer J, Saul L (2005) Distance metric learning for large margin nearest neighbor classification. Annual conference on neural information processing systems
211. Aguiar P, Moura J (2000) Weighted factorization. International conference on image processing pp 549–562
212. Li Y, Brooks M (1999) An efficient recursive factorization method for determining structure from motion. IEEE computer vision and, pattern recognition, pp 138–143
213. Fujiki J, Kurata T (2000) Recursive factorization method for the paraperspective model based on the perspective projection. International conference on, pattern recognition, pp 406–410
214. Fujiki J, Kurata T, Tanaka M (1998) Iterative factorization method for object recognition. International symposium on electronic, imaging, pp 192–201
215. Quan L, Kanade T (1996) A factorization method for affine structure from line correspondences. IEEE computer vision and, pattern recognition, pp 803–808
216. Ueshiba T, Tomita F (1998) A factorization method for projective and Euclidean reconstruction from multiple perspective views via iterative depth estimation. European conference on computer vision pp 296–210
217. Sturm P, Triggs B (1996) A factorization based algorithm for multi-image projective structure and motion. European conference on computer vision, pp 709–720
218. Christy S, Horaud R (1996) Euclidean reconstruction: from paraperspective to perspective. Europ Conf Comp Vis 2:129–140
219. Aguiar P, Moura J (1999) Factorization as a rank 1 problem. IEEE Comp Vis Pattern Recognit 1:178–184
220. Aguiar P, Moura J (1999) A fast algorithm for rigid structure from image sequences. Int Conf Image Proc 3:125–129
221. Aguiar P, Moura J (1998) Video representation via 3D shaped mosaics. Int Conf Image Proc 1:823–827

222. Guerreiro R, Aguiar P (2002) Factorization with missing data for 3D structure recovery. IEEE workshop on multimedia, signal processing, pp 105–108

223. Aguiar P, Moura J (2001) Three-dimensional modeling from two-dimensional video. IEEE Trans Image Proc 10:1541–1551

224. Nakamura K, Saito H, Ozawa S (2000) 3D reconstruction of book surface taken from image sequence with handy camera. Int Conf Pattern Recognit 4:575–578

225. Costeria J, Kanade T (1998) A multi-body factorization method for independently moving objects. Int J Comp Vis 29:159–178

226. Sugaya Y, Kanatani K (2002) Outlier removal for feature tracking by subspace separation. Symposium on sensing via imaging, Info, pp 603–608

227. Huynh D, Hartley R, Heyden A (2003) Outlier correction in image sequences for the affine camera. International conference on computer vision, pp 585–590

228. Huynh D, Heyden A (2001) Outlier detection in video sequences under affine projection. IEEE computer vision and pattern recognition, pp 695–701

229. Ke Q, Kanade T (2003) A robust subspace approach to extracting layers from image sequences. Ph.D. Thesis, Carnegie Mellon University

230. Hawkins D, Liu L, Young S Robust singular value decomposition. http://www.niss.org/technicalreports/tr122.pdf

231. Hwang K, Yokoya N, Takemura H, Yamazawa K (1998) A factorization method using 3-D linear combination for shape and motion recovery. Int Conf Pattern Recognit 2:959–963

232. Yu H, Chen Q, Xu G, Yachida M (1996) 3D shape and motion by SVD under higher-order approximation of perspective projection. International conference on, pattern recognition, pp 456–460

233. Xi L (2004) 3D orthographic reconstruction based on robust factorization method with outliers. International conference on image processing, pp 1927–1930

234. Morita T, Kanade T (1997) A sequential factorization method for recovering shape and motion from image streams. IEEE Trans Pattern Anal Mach Intell 19:858–867

235. Branco C, Costeira J (1998) A 3D image mosaicing system using the factorization method. IEEE Int Symp Ind Electr 2:674–678

236. Guerreiro R, Aguiar P (2002) 3D structure from video streams with partially overlapping images. Int Conf Image Proc 3:897–900

237. Tan J, Ishikawa S (1999) Extracting 3-D motions of individuals at work by uncalibrated multiple video cameras. Int Conf Syst Man Cybern 3:487–490

238. Kurata T, Fujiki J, Kourogi K, Sakaue K (2000) A fast and robust approach to recovering structure and motion from live video frames. IEEE Comp Vis Pattern Recognit 2:528–535

239. Yamaguchi J, Tan J, Ishikawa S (2005) A mobile motion capture system employing image transfer. IEEE TENCON

240. Poelman C, Kanade T (1997) A paraperspective factorization method for shape and motion recovery. IEEE Trans Pattern Anal Mach Intell 19:206–218

241. Tan J, Ishikawa S (2001) Deformable shape recovery by factorization based on a spatiotemporal measurement matrix. Comp Vis Image Underst 82:101–109

242. Tan J, Ishikawa S (2000) On modeling three-dimensional objects by uncalibrated cameras. IEEE TENCON 1:59–63

243. Tomasi C, Kanade T (1992) Shape and motion from image streams under orthography: a factorization method. Int J Comp Vis 9:137–154

244. Djouabi A, Bouktache E (1997) A fast algorithm for the nearest-neighbor classifier. IEEE Trans Pattern Anal Mach Intell 19:277–281

245. Fukunaga K (1985) The estimation of the Bayes error by the k-nearest neighbor approach. In: Kanal L, Rosenfeld A (eds) Progress in pattern recognition, vol 2. Elsevier Science Publishers, London, pp 169–187

246. Forsyth D, Ponce J (2003) Computer vision—a modern approach. Prentice-Hall, Englewood Cliffs

247. Cover T, Hart P (1967) Nearest neighbor pattern classification. IEEE Trans Inf Theory 13:21–27
248. Song Y, Huang J, Zhou D, Zha H, Giles C (2007) IKNN: informative k-nearest neighbor pattern classification. LNAI 4702:248–264
249. Prokop R, Reeves A (1992) A survey of moment-based techniques for unoccluded object representation and recognition. CVGIP: graphical Models Image Proc 54:438–460
250. Dudani S, Breeding K, McGhee R (1977) Aircraft identification by moment invariants. IEEE Trans Comp 26:39–45
251. Sanz P, Marin R, Sanchez J (2005) Including efficient object recognition capabilities in online robots: from a statistical to a neural-network classifier. IEEE Trans SMC Appl Rev 35:87–96
252. Devroye L, Gyorfi L, Lugosi G (1996) A probabilistic theory of pattern recognition. Applications of mathematics—stochastic modelling and applied probability
253. Jozwik A, Serpico S, Roli F (1998) A parallel network of modified 1-NN and k-NN classifiers—application to remote-sensing image classification. Pattern Recognit Lett 19:57–62
254. Sarkar M (2007) Fuzzy-rough nearest neighbor algorithms in classification. Fuzzy Sets Syst 158:2134–2152
255. Bishop C (1995) Neural networks for pattern recognition. Oxford University Press, Oxford
256. Flusser J, Zitova B, Suk T, Moments and moment invariants in image analysis. http://staff.utia.cas.cz/zitova/tutorial/
257. Li Y (1992) Reforming the theory of invariant moments for pattern recognition. Pattern Recognit 25:723–730
258. Maitra S (1979) Moment invariants. IEEE 67:697–699
259. Reiss T (1991) The revised fundamental theorem of moment invariants. EEE Trans Pattern Anal Mach Intell 13:830–834
260. Shutler J, Statistical moments, University of Southampton, UK, Tutorial http://homepages.inf.ed.ac.uk/rbf/CVonline/LOCAL_COPIES/SHUTLER3/CVonline_moments.html
261. Sziranyi T, with other partners UPC, SZTAKI, Bilkent and ACV. Real time detector for unusual behavior. http://www.muscle-noe.org/content/view/147/64/
262. Full-body gesture database. http://gesturedb.korea.ac.kr/
263. Kellokumpu V, Pietikainen M, Heikkila J (2005) Human activity recognition using sequences of postures. Machine vision and applications, pp 570–573
264. Yu S, Tan D, Tan T (2006) A framework for evaluating the effect of view angle, clothing and carrying condition on gait recognition. International conference on, pattern recognition, pp 441–444
265. Sarkar S, Phillips P, Liu Z, Vega I, Grother P, Bowyer K (2005) The humanid gait challenge problem: data sets, performance, and analysis. IEEE Trans Pattern Anal Mach Intell 27:162–177
266. The Inria XMAS (IXMAS) motion acquisition sequences. https://charibdis.inrialpes.fr
267. Ahad A, Ogata T, Tan J, Kim H, Ishikawa S (2007) A smart automated complex motion recognition technique. Workshop on multi-dimensional and multi-view image processing with Asian conference on computer vision, pp 142–149
268. Spengler M, Schiele B (2003) Towards robust multi-cue integration for visual tracking. Mach Vis Appl 14:50–58
269. Piater J, Crowley J (2001) Multi-modal tracking of interacting targets using Gaussian approximations. IEEE workshop on performance evaluation of tracking and surveillance with computer vision and, pattern recognition, pp 141–147
270. Kumar S, Kumar D, Sharma A, McLachlan N (2003) Classification of hand movements using motion templates and geometrical based moments. International conference on intelligent sensing and information processing, pp 299–304
271. Ryu W, Kim D, Lee H, Sung J, Kim D (2006) Gesture recognition using temporal templates. International conference on pattern recognition, demo program

272. Ruiz-del-Solar J, Vallejos P (2004) Motion detection and tracking for an AIBO robot using camera motion compensation and Kalman filtering. RoboCup International Symposium, pp 619–627

273. Valstar M, Patras I, Pantic M (2004) Facial action recognition using temporal templates. IEEE workshop on robot and human interactive, communication, pp 253–258

274. Leman K, Ankit G, Tan T (2005) PDA-based human motion recognition system. Int J Softw Eng Knowl 2:199–205

275. Dollar P, RabaudV, Cottrell G, Belongie S (2005) Behavior recognition via sparse spatiotemporal features. International workshop on visual surveillance and performance evaluation of tracking and surveillance, pp 65–72

276. Shin H, Lee S, Lee S (2005) Real-time gesture recognition using 3D motion history model. Conf Intell Comput LNCS 3644:888–898

277. Davis J (2004) Sequential reliable-inference for rapid detection of human actions. IEEE workshop on detection and recognition of events in video

278. Lo C, Don H (1989) 3-D moment forms: their construction and application to object identification and positioning. IEEE Trans Pattern Anal Mach Intell 11:1053–1063

279. Weinland D, Ronfard R, Boyer E (2006) Automatic discovery of action taxonomies from multiple views. IEEE computer vision and, pattern recognition, pp 1639–1645

280. Canton-Ferrer C, Casas J, Pardas M, Sargin M, Tekalp A (2006) 3D human action recognition in multiple view scenarios. Jornades de Recerca en Automatica, Visi. Robotica

281. Petras I, Beleznai C, Dedeoglu Y, Pardas M et al. (2007) Flexible test-bed for unusual behavior detection. ACM conference image and video retrieval, pp 105–108

282. Dalal N, Triggs B (2005) Histograms of oriented gradients for human detection. IEEE computer vision and, pattern recognition, pp 886–893

283. Dalal D, Triggs B, Schmid C (2006) Human detection using oriented histograms of flow and appearance. European conference on computer vision, pp 428–441

284. Kadir T, Brady M (2001) Scale, saliency and image description. Int J Comp Vis 45(1): 83–105

285. Davis J (1998) Recognizing movement using motion histograms. MIT Media Lab. Perceptual computing section technical report, p 487

286. Senior A, Tosunoglu S (2005) Hybrid machine vision control. Florida conference on recent advances in robotics

287. Wong S, Cipolla R (2005) Continuous gesture recognition using a sparse Bayesian classifier. Int Conf Pattern Recognit 1:1084–1087

288. Wong S, Cipolla R (2005) Real-time adaptive hand motion recognition using a sparse Bayesian classifier. International conference on computer vision, workshop, pp 170–179

289. Ng J, Gong S (2001) Learning pixel-wise signal energy for understanding semantics. British machine vision conference, pp 695–704

290. Ng J, Gong S (2003) Learning pixel-wise signal energy for understanding semantics. Image Vis Comput 21:1183–1189

291. Albu A, Trevor B, Naznin V, Beach C (2007) Analysis of irregularities in human actions with volumetric motion history images. IEEE workshop on motion and video computing

292. Alahari K, Jawahar C (2006) Discriminative actions for recognizing events. Indian conference on computer vision, graphics and image processing, pp 552–563

293. Meng H, Pears N, Freeman M, Bailey C (2009) Motion history histograms for human action recognition. Embedded computer vision (advances in pattern recognition), vol 2. Springer London, pp 139–162

294. Vafadar M, Behrad A (2008) Human hand gesture recognition using motion orientation histogram for interaction of handicapped persons with computer. ICISP. LNCS 5099: 378–385

295. Forbes K (2004) Summarizing motion in video sequences. http://thekrf.com/projects/motion summary/MotionSummary.pdf

296. Tan J, Ishikawa S (2007) High accuracy and real-time recognition of human activities. Annual conference of IEEE industrial electronics society, pp 2377–2382

297. Han J, Bhanu B (2003) Gait energy image representation: comparative performance evaluation on USF HumanID database. Joint international workshop VS-PETS, pp 133–140

298. Han J, Bhanu B (2006) Individual recognition using gait energy image. IEEE Trans Pattern Anal Mach Intell 28(2):133–140

299. Bashir K, Xiang T, Gong S (2008) Feature selection on gait energy image for human identification. IEEE international conference on acoustics, speech and, signal processing, pp 985–988

300. Bashir K, Xiang T, Gong S (2008) Feature selection for gait recognition without subject cooperation. British machine vision conference

301. Yang X, Zhang T, Zhou Y, Yang J (2008) Gabor phase embedding of gait energy image for identity recognition. IEEE international conference on computer and information technology, pp 361–366

302. Chen C, Liang J, Zhao H, Hu H, Tian J (2009) Frame difference energy image for gait recognition with incomplete silhouettes. Pattern Recognit Lett 30(11):977–984

303. Ma Q, Wang S, Nie D, Qiu J (2007) Recognizing humans based on Gait moment image. ACIS international conference on software engineering, artificial intelligence, networking, and parallel/distributed, computing, pp 606–610

304. Yu C, Cheng H, Cheng C, Fan H (2010) Efficient human action and gait analysis using multiresolution motion energy histogram. EURASIP journal on advances in signal processing

305. Ogata T, Tan J, Ishikawa S (2006) High-speed human motion recognition based on a motion history image and an eigenspace. IEICE Trans Inf Syst E89-D(1):281–289

306. Jin T, Leung M, Li L (2004) Temporal human body segmentation. IASTED international conference visualization, imaging, and image processing, pp 1482–7921

307. Singh R, Seth B, Desai U (2006) A real-time framework for vision based human robot interaction. IEEE/RSJ conference on intelligent robots and systems, pp 5831–5836

308. Davis J, Morison A, Woods D (2007) Building adaptive camera models for video surveillance. IEEE workshop on applications of computer vision

309. Ahmad M, Parvin I, Lee S (2010) Silhouette history and energy image information for human movement recognition. J Multimedia 5(1):12–21

310. Watanabe K, Kurita T (2008) Motion recognition by higher orderlocal auto correlation features of motion history images. Bio-inspired, learning and intelligent systems for, security, pp 51–55

311. Chen D, Yan R, Yang J (2007) Activity analysis in privacy-protected video. www.informedia.cs.cmu.edu/documents/T-MM_Privacy_J2c.pdf

312. Ahad A, Tan J, Kim H, Ishikawa S (2010) Action recognition by employing combined directional motion history and energy images. IEEE computer vision and pattern recognition workshop

313. Kindratenko V (1997) Development and application of image analysis techniques for identification and classification of microscopic particles. PhD Thesis, University of Antwerp, Belgium. http://www.ncsa.uiuc.edu/kindr/phd/index.pdf

314. Ahmad M, Hossain M (2008) SEI and SHI representations for human movement recognition. International conference on computer and information technology, pp 521–526

315. Chandrashekhar V, Venkatesh K (2006) Action energy images for reliable human action recognition. Asian symposium on, information display, pp 484–487

316. Chen D, Yang J (2006) Exploiting high dimensional video features using layered Gaussian mixture models. International conference on pattern recognition

317. Meng H, Pears N, Bailey C (2007) A human action recognition system for embedded computer vision application. Workshop on embedded computer vision with computer vision and pattern recognition

318. Meng H, Pears N, Bailey C (2006) Human action classification using SVM_2 K classifier on motion features. Multimedia content representation, classification and security. LNCS 4105:458–465

319. Meng H, Pears N, Bailey C (2007) Motion information combination for fast human action recognition. Conference computer vision theory and applications

320. Meng H, Pears N, Bailey C (2006) Recognizing human actions based on motion information and SVM. IEE international conference intelligent, environments, pp 239–245

321. Babu R, Ramakrishnan K (2003) Compressed domain human motion recognition using motion history information. Int Conf Image Proc 2:321–324

322. Pantic M, Patras I, Valstar M (2005) Learning spatio-temporal models of facial expressions. International conference on measuring, behaviour, pp 7–10

323. Babu R, Ramakrishnan K (2004) Recognition of human actions using motion history information extracted from the compressed video. Image Vis Comput 22:597–607

324. Orrite C, Martinez-Contreras F, Herrero E, Ragheb H, Velastin S (2008) Independent viewpoint silhouette-based human action modelling and recognition. Workshop on machine learning for vision-based motion analysis with European conference on computer vision

325. Jain A, Duin R, Mao J (2000) Statistical pattern recognition: a review. IEEE Trans Pattern Anal Mach Intell 22(1):4–37

326. Shan C, Wei Y, Qiu X, Tan T (2004) Gesture recognition using temporal template based trajectories. Int Conf Pattern Recognit 3:954–957

327. Kellokumpu C, Zhao G, Pietikainen M (2008) Texture based description of movements for activity analysis. Conf Comp Vis Theory Appl 2:368–374

328. Albu A, Beugeling T (2007) A three-dimensional spatiotemporal template for interactive human motion analysis. J Multimedia 2(4):45–54

329. Jan T (2004) Neural network based threat assessment for automated visual surveillance. IEEE Jt Conf Neural Netw 2:1309–1312

330. Liu J, Zhang N (2007) Gait history image: a novel temporal template for gait recognition. IEEE international conference Multimedia and Expo, pp 663–666

331. Xiang T, Gong S (2006) Beyond tracking: modelling activity and understanding behaviour. Int J Comp Vis 67(1):21–51

332. Bobick A, Davis J (1996) An appearance-based representation of action. International conference on, pattern recognition, pp 307–312

333. Davis J (1996) Appearance-based motion recognition of human actions. M.I.T. Media lab perceptual computing group technical report 387

334. Essa I, Pentland S (1995) Facial expression recognition using a dynamic model and motion energy. IEEE computer vision and pattern recognition

335. Haritaoglu I, Harwood D, Davis L (2000) W4: real-time surveillance of people and their activities. IEEE Trans Pattern Anal Mach Intell 22(8):809–830

336. Mittal A, Paragois N (2004) Motion-based background subtraction using adaptive kernel density estimation. IEEE computer vision and pattern recognition

337. Kilger M (1992) A shadow handler in a video-based real-time traffic monitoring system. IEEE workshop on applications of computer vision, pp 1060–1066

338. Yang Y, Levine M (1992) The background primal sketch: an approach for tracking moving objects. Mach Vis Appl 5:17–34

339. Wren C, Azarbayejani A, Darrell T, Pentland A (1997) Pfinder: real-time tracking of the human body. IEEE Trans Pattern Anal Mach Intell 19(7):780–785

340. Stauffer C, Grimson W (1999) Adaptive background mixture models for real-time tracking. IEEE Comp Vis Pattern Recognit 2:246–252

341. McKenna S, Jabri S, Duric Z, Wechsler H, Rosenfeld A (2000) Tracking groups of people. Comp Vis Image Underst 80(1):42–56

342. Arseneau S, Cooperstock J (1999) Real-time image segmentation for action recognition. IEEE pacific rim conference on communications, computers and, signal processing, pp 86–89

343. Sun H, Feng T, Tan T (2000) Robust extraction of moving objects from image sequences. Asian conference on computer vision, pp 961–964
344. Elgammal A, Harwood D, David L (2000) Nonparametric background model for background subtraction. European conference on computer vision
345. Collins R, Lipton A, Kanade T et al (2000) A system for video surveillance and monitoring. Carnegie Mellon University, technical report CMU-RI-TR-00-12
346. Wang C, Brandstein M (1998) A hybrid real-time face tracking system. International conference on acoustics, speech, and signal processing
347. Lipton A, Fujiyoshi H, Patil R (1998) Moving target classification and tracking from real-time video. IEEE workshop on applications of computer vision, pp 8–14
348. Anderson C, Bert P, Wal G (1985) Change detection and tracking using pyramids transformation techniques. SPIE-Intell Robots Comp Vis 579:72–78
349. Bergen J, Burt P, Hingorani R, Peleg S (1992) A three frame algorithm for estimating two-component image motion. IEEE Trans Pattern Anal Mach Intell 14(9):886–896
350. Kameda Y, Minoh M (1996) A human motion estimation method using 3-successive video frames. International conference on virtual systems and multimedia
351. Beauchemin S, Barron J (1995) The computation of optical flow. ACM Comput Surv 27(3):443–467
352. McCane B, Novins K, Crannitch D, Galvin B (2001) On benchmarking optical flow. Comp Vis Image Underst 84:126–143
353. Horn B, Schunck B (1981) Determining optical flow. Artif Intell 17:185–203
354. Papenberg N, Bruhn A, Brox T, Didas S, Weickert J (2006) Highly accurate optic flow computation with theoretically justified warping. Int J Comp Vis 67(2):141–158
355. Wixson L (2000) Detecting salient motion by accumulating directionally-consistent flow. IEEE Trans Pattern Anal Mach Intell 22(8):774–780
356. Talukder A, Goldberg S, Matthies L, Ansar A (2003) Real-time detection of moving objects in a dynamic scene from moving robotic vehicles. IEEE/RSJ international conference on intelligent robots and systems, pp 1308–1313
357. Bimbo A, Nesi P (1993) Real-time optical flow estimation. Int Conf Syst Eng Serv Hum Syst Man Cybern 3:13–19
358. Wei J, Harle N (1997) Use of temporal redundancy of motion vectors for the increase of optical flow calculation speed as a contribution to real-time robot vision. IEEE TENCON, pp 677–680
359. Christmas W (1998) Spatial filtering requirements for gradient-based optical flow. British machine vision conference, pp 185–194
360. Rosales R, Sclaroff S (1999) 3D trajectory recovery for tracking multiple objects and trajectory guided recognition of actions. IEEE Comp Vis Pattern Recognit 2:117–123
361. Zou X, Bhanu B (2006) Human activity classification based on gait energy image and co-evolutionary genetic programming. Int Conf Pattern Recognit 3:555–559
362. Ahmad M, Lee S (2008) Recognizing human actions based on silhouette energy image and global motion description. IEEE automatic face and gesture recognition, pp 523–588
363. Inamura T, Toshima I, Tanie H, Nakamura Y (2004) Embodied symbol emergence based on mimesis theory. Int J Robotics Res 23(4–5):363–377
364. Takano W, Yamane K, Sugihara T, Yamamoto K, Nakamura Y (2006) Primitive communication based on motion recognition and generation with hierarchical mimesis model. International conference on robotics and automation, pp 3602–3608
365. Takano W, Nakamura Y (2006) Humanoid robot's autonomous acquisition of proto-symbols through motion segmentation. IEEE-RAS conference humanoid, robotics pp 425–431
366. Kim T, Park S, Shin S (2003) Rhythmic-motion synthesis based on motion-beat analysis. ACM Trans Graph 22:392–401
367. Shiratori T, Nakazawa A, Ikeuchi K (2004) Detecting dance motion structure through music analysis. IEEE automatic face and gesture recognition, pp 857–862

368. Arikan O, Forsyth D, O'Brien J (2003) Motion synthesis from annotations. ACM Annual Conference Series, Computer Graphics (SIGGRAPH)

369. Bradski G, Davis J (2002) Motion segmentation and pose recognition with motion history gradients. Mach Vis Appl 13(3):174–184

370. Griesbeck C (1996) Introduction to Labanotation. http://user.uni-frankfurt.de/~griesbec/LABANE.html

371. Barbic J, Safonova A, Pan J, Faloutsos C, Hodgins J, Pollard N (2004) Segmenting motion capture data into distinct behaviors. Graphics, interface, pp 185–194

372. Kadone H, Nakamura Y (2006) Segmentation, memorization, recognition and abstraction of humanoid motions based on correlations and associative memory. IEEE-RAS international conference on humanoid robots

373. Peker K, Alatan A, Akansu A (2000) Low-level motion activity features for semantic characterization of video. IEEE conference on Multimedia and Expo, pp 801–804

374. Vitaladevuni S, Kellokumpu V, Davis L (2008) Action recognition using ballistic dynamics. IEEE computer vision and pattern recognition

375. Wang T, Shum H, Xu Y, Zheng N (2001) Unsupervised analysis of human gestures. IEEE pacific rim conference on multimedia, pp 174–181

376. Ihara M, Watanabe N, Nishimura K (1999) A gesture description model based on synthesizing fundamental gestures. IEEE SouthEast conference, pp 47–52

377. Badler N, Costa M, Zhao L, Chi D (2000) To gesture or not to gesture: what is the question? Comp graphics, international, pp 3–9

378. Osaki R, Shimada M, Uehara K (1999) Extraction of primitive motion for human motion recognition. International conference on discovery science, LNCS

379. Mahalingam G, Kambhamettu C (2011) Can discriminative cues aid face recognition across age? IEEE automatic face and gesture recognition

380. Zhang W, Shan S, Qing L, Chen X, Gao W (2009) Are Gabor phases really useless for face recognition? Pattern Anal Appl 12:301–307

381. Guo Y, Zhao G, Chen J, Pietikainen M, Xu Z (2009) A new Gabor phase difference pattern for face and ear recognition. Comp Anal Image Patterns 5702:41–49

382. Perez C, Cament L, Castillo L (2011) Local matching Gabor entropy weighted face recognition. IEEE Autom Face Gesture Recognit

383. Wiskott L, Fellous J, Kruger N, Malsburg C (1997) Face recognition by elastic bunch graph matching. IEEE Trans Pattern Anal Mach Intell 19(7):775–779

384. Liu H (2002) Gabor feature based classification using the enhanced fisher linear discriminant model for face recognition. IEEE Trans Image Proc 11(4):467–476

385. Lei Z, Li S, Chu R, Zhu X (2007) Face recognition with local Gabor textons. International conference on advances in, biometrics pp 49–57

386. Xie S, Shan S, Chen X, Meng X, Gao W (2009) Learned local gabor patterns for face representation and recognition. Signal Proc 89:2333–2344

387. Nguyen H, Bai L, Shen L (2009) Local Gabor binary pattern whitened PCA: a novel approach for face recognition from single image per person. International conference on advances in, biometrics pp 269–278

388. Zou J, Ji Q, Nagy G (2007) A comparative study of local matching approach for face recognition. IEEE Trans Image Proc 16(10):2617–2628

389. Chen Y, De la Torre F (2011) Active conditional models. IEEE automatic face and gesture recognition

390. Leordeanu M, Hebert M (2009) A spectral technique for correspondence problems using pairwise constraints. International conference on computer vision, pp 1482–1489

391. Leordeanu M, Hebert M (2009) Unsupervised learning for graph matching. IEEE computer vision and, pattern recognition, pp 864–871

392. Duchennel O, Bach F, Kweon I, Ponce J (2009) A tensor-based algorithm for high-order graph matching. IEEE computer vision and, pattern recognition, pp 1980–1987

393. Caetano T, McAuley J, Cheng L, Le Q, Smola A (2009) Learning graph matching. IEEE Trans Pattern Anal Mach Intell 31:1048–1058
394. Mikolajczyk K, Tuytelaars T, Schmid C, Zisserman A, Matas J, Schaffalitzky F, Kadir T, Gool L (2005) A comparison of affine region detectors. Int J Comp Vis 65:43–72
395. Zass R, Shashua A (2008) Probabilistic graph and hypergraph matching. IEEE computer vision and pattern recognition
396. Torresani L, Kolmogorov V, Rother C (2008) Feature correspondence via graph matching: models and global optimization. European conference on computer vision, pp 596–609
397. Tola E, Lepetit V, Fua P (2008) A fast local descriptor for dense matching. IEEE computer vision and pattern recognition
398. Ke Y, Sukthankar R (2004) PCA-SIFT: a more distinctive representation for local image descriptors. IEEE computer vision and, pattern recognition, pp 506–513
399. Bay H, Tuytelaars T, Gool L (200) SURF: speeded up robust features. European conference on computer vision, pp 404–417
400. Cootes T, Taylor C, Cooper D, Graham J (1995) Active shape models: their training and application. Comp Vis Image Underst 61:38–59
401. Cootes T, Edwards G, Taylor C (2001) Active appearance models. IEEE Trans Pattern Anal Mach Intell 23:681–685
402. Blanz V, Vetter T (1999) A morphable model for the synthesis of 3D faces. Annual conference on computer graphics and interactive, techniques, pp 187–194
403. Asthana A, Goecke R, Quadrianto N, Gedeon T (2009) Learning-based automatic face annotation for arbitrary poses and expressions from frontal images only. IEEE computer vision and, pattern recognition, pp 1635–1642
404. De la Torre F, Nguyen M (2008) Parameterized kernel principal component analysis: theory and applications to supervised and unsupervised image alignment. IEEE computer vision and pattern recognition
405. Morel J, Yu G (2009) ASIFT—a new framework for fully affine invariant image comparison. SIAM J Image Sci 2:438–469
406. Liu C, Hertzmann A, Popovic Z (2005) Learning physics-based motion style with nonlinear inverse optimization. ACM Trans Graph 24:1071–1081
407. Kohlsdorf D, Starner T, Ashbrook D (2011) MAGIC 2.0: a web tool for false positive prediction and prevention for gesture recognition systems. IEEE automatic face and gesture recognition
408. Ashbrook D, Clawson J, Lyons K, Starner T, Patel N (200) Quickdraw: the impact of mobility and on-body placement on device access time. SIGCHI conference on human factors in, computing systems, pp 219–222
409. Ashbrook D, Starner T (2010) MAGIC: a motion gesture desin tool. CHI, pp 2159–2168
410. Dannenberg A (1989) A gesture based user interface prototyping system. ACM symposium on user interface software and technology
411. Dey A, Hamid R, Beckmann C, Li I, Hsu D (2004) A CAPpella: programming by demonstration of context aware applications. CHI
412. Fails J, Olsen D (2003) A design tool for camera-based interaction. SIGCHI conference on human factors in computing systems
413. Brashear H, Kim J, Lyons K, Starner T, Westeyn T (2007) GART: the gesture and activity recognition toolkit. International conference on human-computer interaction
414. Klemmer S, Sinha A, Chen J, Landay J, Aboobaker N, Wang A (2000) SUEDE: a wizard of oz prototyping tool for speech user interfaces. ACM symposium on user interface software and technology
415. Long A, Landay J, Rowe L (2001) Quill: a gesture design tool for pen-based user interfaces. http://quill.sourceforge.net/
416. Maynes-Aminzade D, Winograd T, Igarashi T (2007) Eyepatch: prototyping camera-based interaction through examples. ACM symposium on user interface software and technology, pp 33–42

417. Akae N, Makihara Y, Yagi Y (2011) The optimal camera arrangement by a performance model for gait recognition. IEEE automatic face and gesture recognition
418. Yu S, Tan D, Tan T (2006) Modelling the effect of view angle variation on appearance-based gait recognition. Conf Comp Vis 1:807–816
419. Makihara Y, Sagawa R, Mukaigawa Y, Echigo T, Yagi Y (2006) Which reference view is effective for gait identification using a view transformation model? IEEE computer society workshop on biometrics
420. Wang Y, Yu S, Wang Y, Tan T (2006) Gait recognition based on fusion of multi-view gait sequences. IAPR international conference on, biometrics, pp 605–611
421. Sugiura K, Makihara Y, Yagi Y (2007) Gait identification based on multi-view observations using omnidirectional camera. Asian conference on computer vision, pp 452–461
422. Mori A, Makihara Y, Yagi Y (2010) Gait recognition using periodbased phase synchronization for low frame-rate videos. International conference on, pattern recognition, pp 2194–2197
423. Mowbray S, Nixon M (2003) Automatic gait recognition via Fourier descriptors of deformable objects. IEEE conference on advanced video and signal based surveillance, pp 566–573
424. Maturana D, Mery D, Soto A (2011).Learning discriminative local binary patterns for face recognition. IEEE automatic face and gesture recognition
425. Mikolajczyk K, Schmid C (2005) Performance evaluation of local descriptors. IEEE Trans Pattern Anal Mach Intell 27(10):1615–1630
426. Liao S, Chung A (2007) Face recognition by using elongated local binary patterns with average maximum distance gradient magnitude. Asian conference on computer vision, pp 672–679
427. Liao S, Zhu X, Lei Z, Zhang L, Li S (2007) Learning multiscale block local binary patterns for face recognition. Advances in, biometrics, pp 828–837
428. Wolf L, Hassner T, Taigman Y (2008) Descriptor based methods in the wild. Real-life images workshop with European conference on computer vision
429. Heikkil M, Pietikinen M, Schmid C (2009) Description of interest regions with local binary patterns. Pattern Recognit 42(3):425–436
430. Xie S, Shan S, Chen X, Gao W (2008) V-LGBP: volume based local gabor binary patterns for face representation and recognition. International conference on pattern recognition
431. Vu N, Caplier A (2010) Face recognition with patterns of oriented edge magnitudes. European conference on computer vision, pp 316–326
432. Park S, Savvides M (2011) The multifactor extension of Grassmann manifolds for face recognition. IEEE automatic face and gesture recognition
433. Li Y, Du Y, Lin X (2005) Kernel-based multifactor analysis for image synthesis and recognition. Int Conf Comp Vis 1:114–119
434. Park S, Savvides M (2007) Individual kernel tensor-subspaces for robust face recognition: a computationally efficient tensor framework without requiring mode factorization. IEEE Trans Syst Man Cybern Cybern 37(5):1156–1166
435. Turk M, Pentland A (1991) Eigenfaces for recognition. J Cogn Neurosci 3:71–86
436. Vasilescu M, Terzopoulos D (2002) Multilinear image analysis for facial recognition. Int Conf Pattern Recognit 1:511–514
437. Vasilescu M, Terzopoulos D (2005) Multilinear independent components analysis. IEEE Comp Vis Pattern Recognit 1:547–553
438. Scholkopf B, Smola A, Muller K (2000) Nonlinear component analysis as a kernel eigenvalue problem. Neural computation, pp 1299–1319
439. O'Hara A, Lui Y, Draper B (2011) Unsupervised learning of human expressions, gestures, and actions. IEEE automatic face and gesture recognition
440. Laptev I (2005) On space-time interest points. Int J Comp Vis 64(2):107–123
441. Rapantzikos K, Avrithis Y, Kollias S (2009) Dense saliency-based spatiotemporal feature points for action recognition. IEEE computer vision and pattern recognition

442. Ponce J, Berg T, Everingham M, Forsyth D, Hebert M, Lazebnik S et al (2006) Dataset issues in object recognition. Toward category-level object recognition. LNCS 4170:29–48
443. Pinto N, DiCarlo J, Cox D (2009) How far can you get with a modern face recognition test set using only simple features? IEEE computer vision and pattern recognition
444. Lv F, Nebatia R (2007) Single view human action recognition using key pose matching and viterbi path searching. IEEE computer vision and pattern recognition
445. Rodriguez M, Ahmed J, Shah M (2008) Action MACH: a spatio-temporal maximum average correlation height filter for action recognition. IEEE computer vision and pattern recognition
446. Yuan C, Li X, Hu W, Wang H (2009) Human action recognition using pyramid vocabulary tree. Asian conference on computer vision
447. Weinland D, Boyer E (2008) Action recognition using exemplar-based embedding. IEEE computer vision and pattern recognition
448. Liu J, Ali S, Shah M (2008) Recognizing human actions using multiple features. IEEE computer vision and pattern recognition
449. Perronnin F (2008) Universal and adapted vocabularies for generic visual categorization. IEEE Trans Pattern Anal Mach Intell 30(7):1243–1256
450. Wang Y, Jiang H, Drew M, Li Z, Mori G (2006) Unsupervised discovery of action classes. IEEE Comp Vis Pattern Recognit
451. Liu J, Shah M (2008) Learning human actions via information maximazation. IEEE computer vision and pattern recognition
452. Fathi A, Mori G (2008) Action recognition by learning mid-level motion features. IEEE computer vision and pattern recognition
453. Jia K, Yeung D (2008) Human action recognition using local spatio-temporal discriminant embedding. IEEE computer vision and pattern recognition
454. Wang L, Suter D (2007) Recognizing human activities from silhouettes: motion subspace and factorial discriminative graphical model. IEEE computer vision and pattern recognition
455. Lucena M, Blanca N, Fuertes J (2010) Human action recognition based on aggregated local motion estimates. Machine vision and applications
456. Brox T, Bruhn A, Papenberg N, Weickert J (2004) High accuracy optical flow estimation based on a theory for warping. European conference on computer vision
457. Bruhn A, Weickert J, Schnorr C (2005) Lucas/Kanade meets Horn/Schunck: combining local and global optic flow methods. Int J Comp Vis 61(3):211–231
458. Farneback C (2003) Two-frame motion estimation based on polynomial expansion. Scandinavian conference on image, analysis, pp 363–370
459. Lucena M, Blanca N, Fuertes J, Marin-Jimenez M (2009) Human action recognition using optical flow accumulated local histograms. IbPRIA, pp 32–39
460. Polana R, Nelson R (1993) Detecting activities. IEEE computer vision and, pattern recognition, pp 2–7
461. Shechtman E, Irani M (2007) Space-time behavior-based correlation or how to tell if two underlying motion fields are similar without computing them? IEEE Trans Pattern Anal Mach Intell 29(11):2045–2056
462. Zelnik-Manor L, Irani M (2001) Event-based analysis of video. IEEE Comp Vis Pattern Recognit 2:123–130
463. Ahmad M, Lee S (2006) HMM-based human action recognition using multiview image sequences. Int Conf Pattern Recognit
464. Babu R, Anantharaman B, Ramakrishnan K, Srinivasan S (2002) Compressed domain action classification using HMM. Pattern Recognit Lett 23(10):1203–1213
465. Brand M, Oliver N, Pentland A (1997) Coupled hidden Markov models for complex action recognition. IEEE computer vision and pattern recognition
466. Cuntoor N, Yegnanarayana B, Chellappa R (2005) Interpretation of state sequences in HMM for activity representation. IEEE ICASSP

467. Mendoza M, Perez de la Blanca N (2007) HMM-based action recognition using contour histograms. Iberian conference on pattern recognition and image analysis

468. Morency L, Quattoni A, Darrell T (2007) Latent-dynamic discriminative models for continuous gesture recognition. M.I.T., technical report

469. Wang S, Quattoni A, Morency L, Demirdjian D, Darrel T (2006) Hidden conditional random fields for gesture recognition. IEEE computer vision and pattern recognition

470. Yamato J, Ohya J, Ishii K (1992) Recognizing human action in time sequential images using hidden Markov model. IEEE computer vision and pattern recognition

471. Mikolajczyk K, Uemura H (2008) Action recognition with motion appearance vocabulary forest. IEEE computer vision and pattern recognition

472. Schindler K, Gool L (2008) Action snippets: how many frames does human action recognition require. IEEE computer vision and pattern recognition

473. Wong S, Cipolla R (2007) Extracting spatiotemporal interest points using global information. International conference on computer vision

474. Kienzle W, Scholkopf B, Wichmann F, Franz M (2007) How to find interesting locations in video: a spatiotemporal interest point detector learned from human eye movements. DAGM Symposium, pp 405–414

475. Bay H, Ess A, Tuytelaars T, Gool L (2008) Speeded-up robust features (SURF). Comp Vis Image Underst 110(3):346–359

476. Kameda Y, Ohta Y (2010) Image retrieval of first-person vision for pedestrian navigation in urban area. International conference on pattern recognition

477. Lindeberg T (1998) Feature detection with automatic scale selection. Int J Comp Vis 30(2):79–116

478. Ehsan S, McDonald-Maier K (2009) Exploring integral image word length reduction techniques for SURF detector. International conference on computer and, electrical engineering, pp 635–639

479. Schweiger F, Zeisl B, Georgel P, Schroth G, Steinbach E, Navab N (2009) Maximum detector response markers for SIFT and SURF. Vision, modeling and visualization workshop

480. BenAbdelkader C, Cutler R, Davis L (2002) Motion-based recognition of people in eigengait space. IEEE automatic face and gesture recognition, pp 378–384

481. Fihl P, Moeslund T (2008) Invariant gait continuum based on the duty-factor. Signal, image and video processing, Springer, London

482. Masoud O, Papanikolopoulos N (2003) A method for human action recognition. Image Vis Comput 21(8):729–743

483. Lee L, Grimson W (2002) Gait analysis for recognition and classification. IEEE automatic face and gesture recognition

484. Zhang R, Vogler C, Metaxas D (2004) Human gait recognition. IEEE computer vision and pattern recognition workshop

485. Ben-Arie J, Wang Z, Pandit P, Rajaram S (2002) Human activity recognition using multidimensional indexing. IEEE Trans Pattern Anal Mach Intell 24(8):1091–1104

486. Rahman M, Ishikawa S (2005) Human motion recognition using an eigenspace. Pattern Recognit Lett 26:687–697

487. Wang L, Tan T, Ning H, Hu W (2003) Silhouette analysis-based gait recognition for human identification. IEEE Trans Pattern Anal Mach Intell 25(12):505–1518

488. Liu Z, Sarkar S (2007) Outdoor recognition at a distance by fusing gait and face. Image Vis Comput 6:817–832

489. Boulgouris V, Plataniotis K, Hatzinakos D (2006) Gait recognition using linear time normalization. Pattern Recognit 39(5):969–979

490. Foster J, Nixon M, Bennett A (2003) Automatic gait recognition using area-based metrics. Pattern Recognit Lett 24(14):2489–2497

491. Andrade E, Fisher R, Blunsden S (2006) Detection of emergency events in crowded scenes. IEE international symposium on imaging for crime detection and, prevention, pp 528–533

492. Bobick A, Davis J (2001) The recognition of human movement using temporal templates. IEEE Trans Pattern Anal Mach Intell 23(3):257–267

493. Efros A, Berg A, Mori G, Malik J (2003) Recognizing action at a distance. International conference on computer vision, pp 726–733

494. Gavrila D (1999) The visual analysis of human movement: a survey. Comp Vis Image Underst 73(1):82–98

495. Grimson W, Stauffer C, Romano R, Lee L (1998) Using adaptive tracking to classify and monitor activities in a site. IEEE computer vision and, pattern recognition, pp 22–29

496. Hu M (1962) Visual pattern recognition by moment invariants. IRE Trans Inf Theory 8(2):179–187

497. Iwai Y, Hata T, Yachida M (1998) Gesture recognition from image motion based on subspace method and HMM. Asian Conf Comp Vis 2:639–646

498. Ke Y, Sukthankar R, Hebert M (2005) Efficient visual event detection using volumetric features. International conference on computer vision, pp 166–173

499. Micilotta A, Ong E, Bowden R (2005) Detection and tracking of humans by probabilistic body part assembly. British machine vision conference, pp 429–438

500. Mitchelson J, Hilton A (2003) Simultaneous pose estimation of multiple people using multiple-view cues with hierarchical sampling. British machine vision conference

501. Robertson N, Reid I (2005) Behaviour understanding in video: a combined method. International conference on computer vision, pp 808–815

502. Roh M, Shin H, Lee S, Lee S (2006) Volume motion template for view-invariant gesture recognition. International conference on, pattern recognition, pp 1229–1232

503. Weinland D, Ronfard R, Boyer E (2005) Motion history volumes for free viewpoint action recognition. IEEE international workshop on modeling people and human interaction

504. Zivkovic Z, Heijden F, Petkovic M, Jonker W (2001) Image processing and feature extraction for recognizing strokes in tennis game videos. Annual conference of the advanced school for computing and, imaging, pp 262–267

505. Aggarwal J, Cai Q (1999) Human motion analysis: a review. Comp Vis Image Underst 73:428–440

506. Aggarwal J, Cai Q (1997) Human motion analysis: a review. IEEE nonrigid and articulated motion, workshop, pp 90–102

507. Bobick A, Intille S, Davis J, Baird F, Pinhanez C, Campbell L et al. (1999) The Kidsroom: a perceptually-based interactive and immersive story environment. Presence Teleoperators Virtual Environ 8:367–391

508. Borshukov G, Bozdagi G, Altunbasak Y, Tekalp A (1997) Motion segmentation by multistage affine classification. IEEE Trans Image Proc 6(11):1591–1594

509. Canton-Ferrer C, Casas J, Pardas M (2006) Human model and motion based 3D action recognition in multiple view scenarios. 14th European signal processing conference

510. Cedras C, Shah M (1995) Motion-based recognition: a survey. Image Vis Comput 13:129–154

511. Davis J (2001) Hierarchical motion history images for recognizing human motion. IEEE workshop on detection and recognition of events in Video, pp 39–46

512. Davis J, Bradski G (1999) Real-time motion template gradients using Intel CVLib. International conference on computer vision workshop on frame-rate vision, pp 1–20

513. Davis J, Bobick A (1998) Virtual PAT: a virtual personal aerobics trainer. Perceptual user, interfaces, pp 13–18

514. Davis J, Bobick A (1997) The representation and recognition of action using temporal templates. IEEE computer vision and, pattern recognition, pp 928–934

515. Gao J, Collins R, Hauptmann A, Wactlar H (2004) Articulated motion modeling for activity analysis. International conference on image and video retrieval, workshop on articulated and nonrigid motion

516. Gheissari N, Bab-Hadiashar A (2003) Motion analysis: model selection and motion segmentation. International conference on image analysis and processing, pp 442–447

517. http://gaijin-in-japan.com/2007/08/11/rajio-taiso-radio-exercise/

518. Hu M (1961) Pattern recognition by moment invariants. IRE 49:1218

519. Kahol K, Tripathi P, Panchanathan P, Rikakis T (2003) Gesture segmentation in complex motion sequences. International conference on image processing, pp 105–108

520. Kahol K, Tripathi P, Panchanathan P (2006) Documenting motion sequences with a personalized annotation system. IEEE J Multimedia 13(1):37–45

521. Kahol K, Tripathi P, Panchanathan P (2004) Automated gesture segmentation from dance sequences. IEEE automatic face and gesture recognitionm, pp 883–888

522. Khotanzad A, Hong Y (1990) Invariant image recognition by Zernike moments. IEEE Trans Pattern Anal Mach Intell 12(5):489–497

523. Li L, Zeng Q, Jiang Y, Xia H (2006) Spatio-temporal motion segmentation and tracking under realistic condition. International symposium on systems and control in aerospace and astronautics, pp 229–232

524. Lo C, Don H (1990) Pattern recognition using 3-D moments. Int Conf Pattern Recognit 1:540–544

525. Mangin J, Poupon F, Duchesnay E, Riviere D et al (2004) Brain morphometry using 3D moments invariants. Med Image Anal 8(3):187–196

526. Rosales R (1998) Recognition of human action using moment-based features. Boston University. Tech Rep 98–020:1–19

527. Shen D, Ip H (1999) Discriminative wavelet shape descriptors for recognition of 2-D patterns. Pattern Recognit 32:151–165

528. Son D, Dinh T, Nam V, Hanh T, Lam H (2005) Detection and localization of road area in traffic video sequences using motion information and Fuzzy-Shadowed sets. IEEE international symposium on multimedia, pp 725–732

529. Teh C, Chin R (1988) On image analysis by the methods of moments. IEEE Trans Pattern Anal Mach Intell 10:496–513

530. Valstar M, Pantic M, Patras I (2004) Motion history for facial action detection in video. Int Conf SMC 1:635–640

531. Weinland D, Ronfard R, Boyer E (2006) Free viewpoint action recognition using motion history volumes. Comp Vis Image Underst 104(2–3):249–257

532. Yau W, Kumar D, Arjunan S, Kumar S (2006) Visual speech recognition using image moments and multiresolution Wavelet. International conference on computer graphics, imaging and visualization, pp 194–199

533. Yau W, Kumar D, Arjunan S (2006) Voiceless speech recognition using dynamic visual speech features. HCSNet workshop use of vision in HCI, pp 39–101

534. Yin Z, Collins R (2006) Moving object localization in thermal imagery by forward-backward MHI. Workshop on object tracking and classification, pp 133–140

535. Yuan C, Medioni G, Kang J, Cohen I (2007) Detecting motion regions in the presence of a strong parallax from a moving camera by multiview geometric constraints. IEEE Trans Pattern Anal Mach Intell 29(9):1627–1641

536. Zhang D, Lu G (2004) Review of shape representation and description techniques. Pattern Recognit 37:1–19

537. Ahad A, Tan J, Kim H, Ishikawa S (2010) A simple approach for low-resolution activity recognition. Int J Comput Vis Biomechanics 3(1):17–24

538. Ahad A, Tan J, Kim H, Ishikawa S (2008) Action recognition with various speeds and timed-DMHI feature vectors. International conference on computer and information technology, pp 213–218

539. Ahad A, Tan J, Kim H, Ishikawa S (2008) Human activity recognition: various paradigms. International conference control, automation and systems, pp 1896–1901

540. Ahad A, Ogata T, Tan J, Kim H, Ishikawa S (2008) Complex motion separation and recognition using directional motion templates. Image analysis—from theory to applications, Research Publishing, Singapore, pp 73–82

541. Ahad A, Uemura H, Tan J, Kim H, Ishikawa S (2008) A simple real-time approach for action separation into action primitives. International workshop on tracking humans for the evaluation of their motion in image sequences with british machine vision conference, pp 69–78

542. Ahad A, Tan J, Kim H, Ishikawa S (2009) Temporal motion recognition and segmentation approach. Int J Imag Syst Technol 19:91–99

543. Ahad A, Tan J, Kim H, Ishikawa S (2010) Analysis of motion self-occlusion problem due to motion overwriting for human activity recognition. J Multimedia 5(1):36–46

544. Ahad A, Tan J, Kim H, Ishikawa S (2008) Solutions to motion self-occlusion problem in human activity analysis. International conference on computer and information technology, pp 201–206

545. Ahad A, Tan J, Kim H, Ishikawa S (2008) Directional motion history templates for low resolution motion recognition. Annual conference of the IEEE industrial electronics society (IECON), pp 1875–1880

546. Sigal L, Black M (2006) HumanEva: Synchronized video and motion capture dataset for evaluation of articulated human motion. Department of Computer Science, Brown University, technical report CS-06-08

547. Moeslund T (1999) Summaries of 107 computer vision-based human motion capture papers. University of Aalborg, technical report LIA 99–01

548. Zhou H, Hu H (2004) A survey-human movement tracking and stroke rehabilitation. Department of Computer Sciences, University of Essex, technical report CSM-420

549. Pavlovic V, Sharma R, Huang T (1997) Visual interpretation of hand gestures for human-computer interaction: a review. IEEE Trans Pattern Anal Mach Intell 19(7):677–695

550. Pantic M, Pentland A, Nijholt A, Hunag T (2006) Human computing and machine understanding of human behavior: a survey. International conference on multimodal interface, pp 239–248

551. Pantic M, Pentland A, Nijholt A, Hunag T (2007) Human computing and machine understanding of human behavior: a survey. Hum Comput LNAI 4451:47–71

552. Marcel S (2002) Gestures for multi-modal interfaces: a review. IDIAP research, report 02–34

553. Tangelder J, Veltkamp R (2004) A survey of content based 3D shape retrieval methods. Shape modeling applications, pp 145–156

554. LaViola J (1999) A survey of hand posture and gesture recognition techniques and technology. Brown University, technical report CS-99-11

555. Jaimes A, Sebe N (2007) Multimodal human-computer interaction: a survey. Comp Vis Image Underst 108(1–2):116–134

556. Varga E, Horvath I, Rusak Z, Broek J (2004) Hand motion processing in applications: a concise survey and analysis of technologies. International design conference

557. Poppe R (2007) Vision-based human motion analysis: an overview. Comp Vis Image Underst 108(1–2):4–18

558. Moeslund T, Hilton A, Kruger V (2006) A survey of advances in vision-based human motion capture and analysis. Comp Vis Image Underst 104:90–126

559. Wang J, Singh S (2003) Video analysis of human dynamics—a survey. Real-Time Imag 9(5):321–346

560. Buxton H (2003) Learning and understanding dynamic scene activity: a review. Image Vis Comput 21(1):125–136

561. Aggarwal J, Park S (2004) Human motion: modeling and recognition of actions and interactions. International symposium on 3D data processing, visualization and transmission, pp 640–647

562. Prati A, Mikic I, Trivedi M, Cucchiara R (2003) Detecting moving shadows: algorithms and evaluation. IEEE Trans Pattern Anal Mach Intell 25(7):918–923

563. Mitra S, Acharya T (2007) Gesture recognition: a survey. IEEE Trans SMC 37(3):311–324

564. Moeslund T, Granum E (2001) A survey of computer vision-based human motion capture. Comp Vis Image Underst 81:231–268

565. Hu W, Tan T, Wang L, Maybank S (2004) A survey on visual surveillance of object motion and behaviors. IEEE Trans SMC Appl Rev 34(3):334–352

566. Boulay B, Bremond F, Thonnat M (2006) Applying 3D human model in a posture recognition system. Pattern Recognit Lett 27:1788–1796

567. Wang L, Hu W, Tan T (2003) Recent developments in human motion analysis. Pattern Recognit 36:585–601

568. Joshi M (2006) Digital image processing—an algorithmic approach. Prentice-Hall, India

569. Teknomo K, Tutorial on normalization methods. http://people.revoledu.com/kardi/tutorial/Similarity/Normalization.html

570. Dubes R (2009) Cluster analysis and related issues. Handbook of pattern recognition and computer vision, 4th edn. World scientific, pp 3–32

571. Davis J, Tyagi A (2006) Minimal-latency human action recognition using reliable-inference. Image Vis Comput 24:455–472

572. Chen H, Chen H, Chen Y, Lee S (2006) Human action recognition using star skeleton. ACM international workshop on video surveillance and sensor, networks, pp 171–174

573. Jin N, Mukhtarian F (2006) A non-parametric HMM learning method for shape dynamics with application to human motion recognition. Int Conf Pattern Recognit 2:29–32

574. Kulic D, Takano W, Nakamura Y (2007) Representability of human motions by Factorial Hidden Markov Models. IEEE/RSJ international conference on intelligent robots and systems, pp 2388–2393

575. Peursum P, Bui H, Venkatesh S, West G (2005) Robust recognition and segmentation of human actions using HMMs with missing observations. EURASIP J Appl Signal Proc 2005(1):2110–2126

576. Song S, Xing T (2003) Recognition of group activities using dynamic probabilistic networks. Int Conf Comp Vis 2:742–749

577. Sminchisescu C, Kanaujia A, Li Z, Metaxas D (2005) Conditional models for contextual human motion recognition. Int Conf Comp Vis 2:1808–1815

578. Nguyen N, Phung D, Venkatesh S, Bui H (2006) Learning and detecting activities from movement trajectories using the Hierarchical Hidden Markov Models. IEEE computer vision and, pattern recognition, pp 955–960

579. Park S, Aggarwal J (2004) Semantic-level understanding of human actions and interactions using event hierarchy. International workshop with IEEE computer vision and, pattern recognition, pp 12–20

580. Ryoo M, Aggarwal J (2006) Recognition of composite human activities through context-free grammar based representation. IEEE computer vision and, pattern recognition, pp 1709–1718

581. Shi Y, Huang Y, Minnen D, Bobick A, Essa I (2004) Propagation networks for recognition of partially ordered sequential action. IEEE computer vision and, pattern recognition, pp 862–869

582. Shi Y, Bobick A, Essa I (2006) Learning temporal sequence model from partially labeled data. IEEE computer vision and, pattern recognition, pp 1631–1638

583. Ahmad M, Lee S (2006) Human action recognition using multi-view image sequences features. IEEE automatic face and gesture recognition, pp 523–528

584. Leo M, D'Orazio T, Gnoni I, Spagnolo P, Distante A (2004) Complex human activity recognition for monitoring wide outdoor environments. International conference on, pattern recognition, pp 913–916

585. Davis J, Gao H (2003) Recognizing human action efforts: an adaptive three-mode PCA framework. International conference on computer vision, pp 1463–1469

586. Troje N (2002) Decomposing biological motion: a framework for analysis and synthesis of human gait patterns. J Vis 2:371–387

587. Davis J, Gao H (2004) Gender recognition from walking movements using adaptive three-mode PCA. IEEE computer vision and pattern recognition workshop

588. Fanti C, Zelnik-Manor L, Perona P (2005) Hybrid models for human motion recognition. IEEE computer vision and, pattern recognition, pp 1166–1173
589. Song Y, Goncalves L, Perona P (2003) Unsupervised learning of human motion. IEEE Trans Pattern Anal Mach Intell 25(7):814–827
590. Parameswaran V, Chellappa R (2005) Human action-recognition using mutual invariants. Comp Vis Image Underst 98(2):295–325
591. Yilmaz A, Shah M (2006) Matching actions in presence of camera motion. Comp Vis Image Underst 104(2):221–231
592. Uemura H, Ishikawa S, Mikolajczyk M (2008) Feature tracking and motion compensation for action recognition. British machine vision conference
593. Bodor R, Jackson B, Masoud O, Papanikolopoulos N (2003) Image-based reconstruction for view-independent human motion recognition. IEEE/RSJ international conference on intelligent robots and systems, pp 1548–1553
594. Rao C, Yilmaz A, Shah M (2002) View-invariant representation and recognition of actions. Int J Comp Vis 50(2):203–226
595. Ali S, Basharat A, Shah M (2007) Chaotic invariants for human action recognition. International conference on computer vision
596. Lai Y, Liao H (2006) Human motion recognition using clay representation of trajectories. International conference on intelligent info hiding and multimedia, signal processing, pp 335–338
597. Dewaele G, Cani M (2003) Interactive global and local deformations for virtual clay. Pacific conference on computer graphics and applications, pp 131–140
598. Zelnik-Manor L, Irani M (2006) Statistical analysis of dynamic actions. IEEE Trans Pattern Anal Mach Intell 28(9):1530–1535
599. Loy G, Sullivan J, Carlsson S (2003) Pose-based clustering in action sequences. IEEE international workshop on higher-level knowledge in 3D modeling and motion, analysis, pp 66–73
600. Gorelick L, Galun M, Sharon E, Brandt A, Basri R (2006) Shape representation and classification using the poisson equation. IEEE Trans Pattern Anal Mach Intell 28(12)
601. Gorelick L, Blank M, Shechtman E, Irani M, Basri R (2007) Actions as space-time shapes. IEEE Trans Pattern Anal Mach Intell 29(12):2247–2253
602. Blank M, Gorelick L, Shechtman E, Irani M, Basri R (2005) Actions as space-time shapes. International conference on computer vision, pp 1395–1402
603. Shechtman E, Irani M (2005) Space-time behavior based correlation. IEEE computer vision and, pattern recognition, pp 405–412
604. Viola P, Jones M, Snow D (2003) Detecting pedestrians using patterns of motion and appearance. International conference on computer vision, pp 734–742
605. Oikonomopoulos A, Patras I, Pantic M (2006) Spatiotemporal salient points for visual recognition of human actions. IEEE Trans SMC 36(3):710–719
606. Laptev I, Lindeberg T (2004) Velocity adaptation of space-time interest points. International conference on pattern recognition
607. Rittscher J, Blake A, Roberts S (2002) Towards the automatic analysis of complex human body motions. Image Vis Comput 20:905–916
608. Yilmaz A, Shah M (2005) Actions sketch: a novel action representation. IEEE computer vision and, pattern recognition, pp 984–989
609. Bobick A, Wilson A (1997) A state-based approach to the representation and recognition of gesture. IEEE Trans Pattern Anal Mach Intell 19(12):1325–1337
610. Dong Q, Wu Y, Hu Z (2006) Gesture recognition using quadratic curves. Asian conference on computer vision, pp 817–825
611. Shin M, Tsap L, Goldgof D (2004) Gesture recognition using Bezier curves for visualization navigation from registered 3-D data. Pattern Recognit 37(5):1011–1024
612. Wang L, Suter D (2006) Informative shape representations for human action recognition. International conference on, pattern recognition, pp 1266–1269

613. Zhong H, Shi J, Visontai M (2004) Detecting unusual activity in video. IEEE computer vision and, pattern recognition, pp 819–826
614. Boiman O, Irani M (2005) Detecting irregularities in images and in video. International conference on computer vision, pp 462–469
615. Xiang T, Gong S (2005) Video behaviour profiling and abnormality detection without manual labelling. International conference on computer vision, pp 1238–1245
616. Cuntoor N, Chellappa R (2007) Epitomic representation of human activities. IEEE computer vision and, pattern recognition, pp 846–853
617. Harris C, Stephens M (1988) A combined corner and edge detector. Alvey vision conference, pp 147–151
618. Lowe D (2004) Distinctive image features from scale-invariant keypoints. Int J Comp Vis 60(2):91–110
619. Lucas B, Kanade T (1981) An iterative image registration technique with an application to stereo vision. International joint conference, artificial intelligence, pp 674–679
620. Dong Q, Wu Y, Hu Z (2009) Pointwise motion image (PMI): a novel motion representation and its applications to abnormality detection and behavior recognition. IEEE Trans Circuits Syst Video Technol 19(3):407–416
621. Cox D, Pinto N (2011) Beyond simple features: a large-scale feature search approach to unconstrained face recognition. IEEE automatic face and gesture recognition
622. Pinto N, Cox D, DiCarlo J (2008) Why is real-world visual object recognition hard. PLoS computational biology
623. Pinto N, DiCarlo J, Cox D (2008) Establishing good benchmarks and baselines for face recognition. European conference on computer vision
624. Pinto N, Doukhan D, DiCarlo J, Cox D (2009) A high-throughput screening approach to discovering good forms of biologically inspired visual representation.PLoS computational biology
625. Shreve M, Godavarthy S, Goldgof D, Sarkar S (2011) Macro- and micro-expression spotting in long videos using spatio-temporal strain. IEEE Autom Face Gesture Recognit
626. Ekman P (2001) Telling lies: clues to deceit in the marketplace, politics, and marriage. W.W, Norton and Company
627. Ekman P, Rolls E, Perrett D, Ellis H (1992) Facial expressions of emotion: an old controversy and new findings [and discussion]. Philos Trans Biological Sci 335:63–69
628. Luu K, Bui T, Suen C (2011) Kernel spectral regression of perceived age from hybrid facial features. IEEE automatic face and gesture recognition
629. Tan X, Triggs B (2010) Enhanced local texture feature sets for face recognition under difficult lighting conditions. IEEE Trans Image Proc 19(6):1635–1650
630. Ahonen T, Hadid A, Pietikainen M (2004) Face recognition with local binary patterns. European conference on computer vision, pp 469–481
631. Ahonen T, Hadid A, Pietikainen M (2006) Face description with local binary patterns: application to face recognition. IEEE Trans Pattern Anal Mach Intell 28(12):2037–2041
632. Lui Y, Beveridge J (2011) Tangent bundle for human action recognition. IEEE automatic face and gesture recognition
633. Ben-Yosef G, Ben-Shahar O (2010) Minimum length in the tangent bundle as a model for curve completion. IEEE computer vision and pattern recognition
634. Conway J, Hardin R, Sloane N (1996) Packing lines, planes, etc.: Packings in grassmannian spaces. Exp Math 5(2):139–159
635. Kim T, Cipolla R (2007) Gesture recognition under small sample size. Asian conference on computer vision
636. Kim T, Cipolla R (2009) Canonical correlation analysis of video volume tensors for action categorization and detection. IEEE Trans Pattern Anal Mach Intell 31(8):1415–1428
637. Kovashka A, Grauman K (2010) Learning a hierarchy of discriminative space-time neighborhood features for human action recognition. IEEE computer vision and pattern recognition

638. Laptev I, Marszalek M, Schmid C, Rozenfield B (2008) Learning realistic human actions from movies. IEEE computer vision and pattern recognition
639. Li R, Chellappa R (2010) Aligning spatio-temporal signals on a special manifold. European conference on computer vision
640. Lin Z, Jiang Z, Davis L (2009) Recognizing actions by shape-motion prototype trees. International conference on computer vision
641. Lui Y, Beveridge J, Kirby M (2009) Canonical stiefel quotient and its application to generic face recognition in illumination spaces. IEEE international conference biometrics: theory, applications, and systems, pp 1–8
642. Lui Y, Beveridge J, Kirby M (2010) Action classification on product manifolds. IEEE computer vision and pattern recognition
643. Niebles J, Wang H, Fei-Fei L (2008) Unsupervised learning of human action categories using spatial-temporal words. Int J Comp Vis 79(3):299–318
644. Silva J, Marques J, Lemos J (2005) Non-linear dimension reduction with tangent bundle approximation. ICASSP
645. Veeraraghavan A, Roy-Chowdhury A, Chellappa R (2005) Matching shape sequences in video with applications in human movement analysis. IEEE Trans Pattern Anal Mach Intell 12:1896–1909
646. Wang H, Ullah M, Klaser A, Laptev I, Schmid C (2009) Evaluation of local spatio-temporal features for action recognition. British machine vision conference
647. Edelman A, Arias R, Smith S (1999) The geometry of algorithms with orthogonal constraints. SIAM J Matrix Anal Appl 2:303–353
648. Kendall D (1984) Shape manifolds, procrustean metrics and complex projective spaces. Bull Lond Math Soc 16:81–121
649. Oshin O, Gilbert A, Bowden R (2011) Capturing the relative distribution of features for action recognition. IEEE automatic face and gesture recognition
650. Blake R, Shiffrar M (2007) Perception of human motion. Ann Rev Psychol 58:47–73
651. Schuldt C, Laptev I, Caputo B (2004) Recognizing human actions: a local SVM approach. International conference on pattern recognition
652. Dollar P, Rabaud V, Cottrell G, Belongie S (2005) Behavior recognition via sparse spatio-temporal features. VS-PETS
653. Liu J, Luo J, Shah M (2009) Recognizing realistic actions from videos. IEEE computer vision and pattern recognition
654. Gilbert A, Illingworth J, Bowden R (2009) Fast realistic multi-action recognition using mined dense spatio-temporal features. International conference on computer vision
655. Laptev I, Lindeberg T (2003) Space-time interest points. International conference on computer vision
656. Willems G, Tuytelaars T, Gool L (2008) An efficient dense and scale-invariant spatio-temporal interest point detector. European conference on computer vision
657. Scovanner P, Ali S, Shah M (2007) A 3-dimensional sift descriptor and its application to action recognition. International conference on multimedia, pp 357–360
658. Klaser A, Marszalek M, Schmid C (2008) A spatio-temporal descriptor based on 3D-gradients. British machine vision conference
659. Laptev I, Perez P (2007) Retrieving actions in movies. International conference on computer vision
660. Marszalek M, Laptev I, Schmid C (2009) Actions in context. IEEE computer vision and pattern recognition
661. Ryoo M, Aggarwal J (2009) Spatio-temporal relationship match: video structure comparison for recognition of complex human activities. international conference on computer vision
662. Matikainen P, Herbert M, Sukthankar R (2010) Representing pairwise spatial and temporal relations for action recognition. European conference on computer vision

663. Savarese S, DelPozo A, Niebles J, Fei-Fei L (2008) Spatial-temporal correlatons for unsupervised action classification. WMVC
664. Cui Z, Shan S, Chen X, Zhang L (2011) Sparsely encoded local descriptor for face recognition. IEEE automatic face and gesture recognition
665. Zhao G, Pietikinen M (2006) Local binary pattern descriptors for dynamic texture recognition. International conference on, pattern recognition, pp 211–214
666. Zhang B, Shan S, Chen X, Gao W (2007) Histogram of Gabor phase patterns (HGPP): a novel object representation approach for face recognition. IEEE Trans Image Proc 16(1):57–68
667. Zhang W, Shan S, Gao W, Chen X, Zhang H (2005) Local Gabor binary pattern histogram sequence (LGBPHS): a novel non-statistical model for face representation and recognition. International conference on computer vision
668. Xie S, Shan S, Chen X, Chen J (2010) Fusing local patterns of Gabor magnitude and phase for face recognition. IEEE Trans Image Proc 19(5):1349–1361
669. Bicego M, Lagorio A, Grosso E, Tistarelli M (2006) On the use of SIFT features for face authentication. IEEE computer vision and pattern recognition workshop
670. Albiol A, Monzo D, Martin A, Sastre J, Albiol A (2008) Face recognition using HOG-EBGM. Pattern Recognit Lett 29:1537–1543
671. Gorodnichy D (2005) Associative neural networks as means for low-resolution video-based recognition. International joint conference on neural networks
672. Kong W, Zhang D (2002) Palmprint texture analysis based on low-resolution images for personal authentication. International conference on, pattern recognition, pp 807–810
673. Sobottka K (2000) Analysis of low-resolution range image sequences. PhD Thesis
674. Roh M, Christmas W, Kittler J, Lee S (2006) Robust player gesture spotting and recognition in low-resolution sports video. European conference on computer vision, pp 347–358
675. Lee S, Park J, Lee S (2006) Low resolution face recognition based on support vector data description. Pattern Recognit 39:1809–1812
676. Yanadume S, Mekada Y, Ide I, Murase H (2004) Recognition of very low-resolution characters from motion images captured by a portable digital camera. Advances in multimedia information processing, pp 247–254
677. Nomura M, Yamamoto K, Ohta H, Kato K (2005) A proposal of the effective recognition method for low-resolution characters from motion images. Int Conf Document Anal Recognit 2:720–724
678. Wu H, Chen H, Wu R, Shen D (2006) License plate extraction in low resolution video.International conference on, pattern recognition, pp 824–827
679. Bo N, Dailey M, Uyyanonvara B (2007) Robust hand tracking in low-resolution video sequences. IASTED international conference on advances in computer, science and technology, pp 228–233
680. Roh M, Christmas W, Kittler J, Lee S (2008) Gesture spotting for low-resolution sports video annotation. Pattern Recognit 41(3):1124–1137
681. Jun K, Kunihito K, Kazuhiko Y (1999) Character recognition at low resolution with video camera. J Inst Image Inf Telev Eng 53(6):867–872
682. Cutler R, Davis L (2000) Robust real-time periodic motion detection: analysis and applications. IEEE Trans Pattern Anal Mach Intell 22:781–796
683. Pittermann J, Pittermann A, Minker W (2010) Human emotions. Handling emotions in human-computer dialogues, pp 19–45
684. Kim J, Hill R, Durlach P, Lane H, Forbell E, Core M et al (2009) BiLAT: a game-based environment for practicing negotiation in a cultural context. Int J Artif Intell Educ 19(3):289–308
685. Peursum P, Bui H, Venkatesh S, West G (2004) Human action recognition with an incomplete real-time pose skeleton. Curtin University of Technology, Australia, technical report 2004/1

686. Griffiths P (2001) Emotion and expression. International encyclopedia of the social & behavioral sciences, pp 4433–4437
687. Baillie L, Morton L, Moffat D, Uzor S (2010) Capturing the response of players to a location-based game. Personal and ubiquitous computing
688. Wang N, Marsella S (2006) Introducing EVG: an emotion evoking game. LNCS 4133: 282–291
689. Baillie L, Morton L, Moffat D, Uzor S (2010) An investigation of user responses to specifically designed activities in a multimodal location based game. J Multimodal User Interf 3(3):179–188
690. Albrecht I, Schroder M, Haber J, Seidel H (2005) Mixed feelings: expression of non-basic emotions in a muscle-based talking head. Virtual Real 8:201–212
691. Ekman P, Keltner D (1997) Universal facial expressions of emotion: an old controversy and new findings. Nonverbal communication: where nature meets culture, Lawrence Erlbaum Associates Inc., Mahwah, pp 27–46
692. Wang N, Marsella S, Hawkins T (2008) Individual differences in expressive response: a challenge for ECA design. International joint conference on autonomous agents and multiagent systems
693. Leite I, Martinho C, Pereira A, Paiva A (2008) iCat: an affective game buddy based on anticipatory mechanisms. International conference on autonomous agents and multiagent systems, pp 1229–1232
694. Nguyen Q, Novakowski S, Boyd J, Jacob C, Hushlak G (2006) Motion swarms: video interaction for art in complex environments. ACM international conference multimedia, pp 461–469
695. Peursum P, Bui H, Venkatesh S, West G (2004) Classifying human actions using an incomplete real-time pose skeleton. LNCS 3157:971–972
696. Fujiyoshi H, Lipton A (1999) Real-time human motion analysis by image skeletonization. Workshop on application of computer vision
697. Li W, Zhang Z, Liu Z (2010) Action recognition based on a bag of 3D points. IEEE computer vision and pattern recognition workshop
698. Wang X, Han T, Yan S (2009) An HOG-LBP human detector with partial occlusion handling. International conference on computer vision
699. Canny J (1986) A computational approach to edge detection. IEEE Trans Pattern Anal Mach Intell 8(6):679–698
700. Ahad A, Tan J, Kim H, Ishikawa S (2010) Motion history image: its variants and applications. Mach Vis Appl. doi:10.1007/s00138-010-0298-4
701. Gafurov D (2007) A survey of biometric gait recognition: approaches, security and challenges. NIK conference
702. Tao Y, Grosky W (1999) Object-based image retrieval using point feature maps. International conference on database semantics, pp 59–73
703. Shahabi C, Safar M (2006) An experimental study of alternative shape-based image retrieval techniques. Multimedia Tools Appl. doi:10.1007/s11042-006-0070-y
704. Samma A, Salam R (2009) Enhancement of shape description and representation by slope. World academy of science, engineering and technology, p 59
705. Blostein S, Huang T (1991) Detecting small, moving objects in image sequences using sequential hypothesis testing. IEEE Trans Signal Proc 39(7):1611–1629
706. Meir R, Ratsch G (2003) An introduction to boosting and leveraging. Adv Lectures Mach Learn 2600:119–184
707. Freund Y (1990) Boosting a weak learning algorithm by majority. Workshop on computational learning theory
708. Wang H (2011) Structural two-dimensional principal component analysis for image recognition. Mach Vis Appl 22:433–438
709. Ahad MAR (2011) Computer vision and action recognition, Atlantis Press

710. Thi T, Cheng L, Zhang J, Wang L (2010) Implicit motion-shape model: a generic approach for action matching. In: Proceedings of IEEE international conference on image processing
711. Tian Y, Cao L, Liu Z, Zhang Z (2011) Hierarchical filtered motion for action recognition in crowded videos IEEE transactions on systems, Man, and Cybernetics—Part C
712. Akyol S, Alvarado P (2001) Finding relevant image content for mobile sign language recognition. In: Proceedings of the IASTED international conference signal processing, pattern recognition and applications, pp 48–52
713. Tanawongsuwan R, Stoytchev A, Essa I (1999) Robust tracking of people by a mobile robotic agent, technical report, Georgia Institute of Technology. http://smartech.gatech.edu/handle/1853/3386
714. Brown D, Ghaziasgar M, Connan J (2012) Automated suspicious activity detection. In: Proceedings of Southern Africa telecommunication networks and applications conference (SATNAC)
715. Briassouli A, Kompatsiaris I (2009) Robust temporal activity templates using higher order statistics, IEEE Trans Image proc 18(12)
716. Alvarez L, Esclarín J, Lefébure M, Sánchez J (1999) A PDE model for computing the optical flow. In Proceeding XVI Congreso de Ecuaciones Diferenciales y Aplicaciones, Las Palmas de Gran Canaria, Spain, pp 1349–1356
717. Aubert G, Deriche R, Kornprobst P (1999) Computing optical flow via variational techniques. SIAM J Appl Math 60(1):156–182
718. Black MJ, Anandan P (1991) Robust dynamic motion estimation over time. In: Proceedings 1991 IEEE computer society conference on computer vision and pattern recognition. IEEE Computer Society Press, Maui, pp 292–302
719. Cohen I (1993) Nonlinear variational method for optical flow computation. In: Proceedings eighth scandinavian conference on image analysis, vol 1. Tromsø, Norway, pp 523–530
720. Deriche R, Kornprobst P, Aubert G (1995) Optical-flow estimation while preserving its discontinuities: a variational approach. In: Proceedings second asian conference on computer vision, vol 2. Singapore, pp 290–295
721. Heitz F, Bouthemy P (1993) Multimodal estimation of discontinuous optical flow using Markov random fields. IEEE Trans Pattern Anal Mach Intell 15(12):1217–1232
722. Kumar A, Tannenbaum AR, Balas GJ (1996) Optic flow: a curve evolution approach. IEEE Trans Image Proc 5(4):598–610
723. Nagel H–H (1983) Constraints for the estimation of displacement vector fields from image sequences. In: Proceedings eighth international joint conference on artificial intelligence, vol 2. Karlsruhe, West Germany, pp 945–951
724. Nesi P (1993) Variational approach to optical flow estimation managing discontinuities. Image Vis Comput 11(7):419–439
725. Proesmans M et al (1994) Determination of optical flow and its discontinuities using non-linear diffusion. In Computer vision–ECCV'94, Eklundh J-O (ed) Lecture notes in computer science, vol 801. Springer, Berlin, pp 295–304
726. Schnörr C (1994) Segmentation of visual motion by minimizing convex non-quadratic functionals. In: Proceedings twelfth international conference on pattern recognition, vol A. Jerusalem, Israel, IEEE Computer Society Press, pp 661–663
727. Weickert J, Schnörr C (2001) Variational optic flow computation with a spatio-temporal smoothness constraint. J Math Imag Vis 14(3):245–255
728. Farnebäck G (2001) Very high accuracy velocity estimation using orientation tensors, parametric motion, and simultaneous segmentation of the motion field. In: Proceeding eighth international conference on computer vision, vol 1. IEEE Computer Society Press, Vancouver, Canada, pp 171–177
729. Mémin E, Pérez P (2002) Hierarchical estimation and segmentation of dense motion fields. Int J Comp Vis 46(2):129–155

730. Cremers D (2003) A multiphase levelset framework for variational motion segmentation. In: GriffinLD, Lillholm M (ed) Scale space methods in computer vision, Lecture notes in computer science, vol 2695. Springer, Berlin, pp 599–614

731. Black MJ, Jepson A (1996) Estimating optical flow in segmented images using variable-order parametric models with local deformations. IEEE Trans Pattern Anal Mach Intell 18(10):972–986

732. Anandan P (1989) A computational framework and an algorithm for the measurement of visual motion. Int J Comp Vis 2:283–310

733. Mémin E, Pérez P (1998) A multigrid approach for hierarchical motion estimation. In: Proceedings sixth international conference on computer vision. Narosa Publishing House, Bombay, India, pp 933–938

734. Nagel H-H, Enkelmann W (1986) An investigation of smoothness constraints for the estimation of displacement vector fields from image sequences. IEEE Trans Pattern Anal Mach Intell 8:565–593

735. Alvarez L, Weickert J, Sánchez J (2000) Reliable estimation of dense optical flow fields with large displacements. Int J Comp Vis 39(1):41–56

736. Nagel H-H (1990) Extending the oriented smoothness constraint into the temporal domain and the estimation of derivatives of optical flow. In: Faugeras O (ed) Computer vision, Lecture notes in computer science, vol 427. Springer, Berlin, 139–148

737. Murray DW, Buxton BF (1987) Scene segmentation from visual motion using global optimization. IEEE Trans Pattern Anal Mach Intell 9(2):220–228

738. Elad M, Feuer A (1998) Recursive optical flow estimation–adaptive filtering approach. J Vis Commun Image Represent 9(2):119–138

739. Chiu WY, Tsai DM (2010) A macro-observation scheme for abnormal event detection in daily-life video sequences. EURASIP J Adv Signal Proc. http://dl.acm.org/citation.cfm?id=1928533

740. http://marathon.csee.usf.edu/GaitBaseline/

741. http://www.cse.ohio-state.edu/~jwdavis/CVL/Research/MHI/mhi.html

742. http://www-staff.it.uts.edu.au/~massimo/BackgroundSubtractionReview-Piccardi.pdf

743. Liu J, Shah M, Kuipers B, Savarese S (2011) Cross-view action recognition via view knowledge transfer. In: Proceedings of IEEE conference CVPR

Index

Md. A. R. Ahad, *Motion History Images for Action Recognition and Understanding*, 119
SpringerBriefs in Computer Science, DOI: 10.1007/978-1-4471-4730-5,
© Md. Atiqur Rahman Ahad 2013